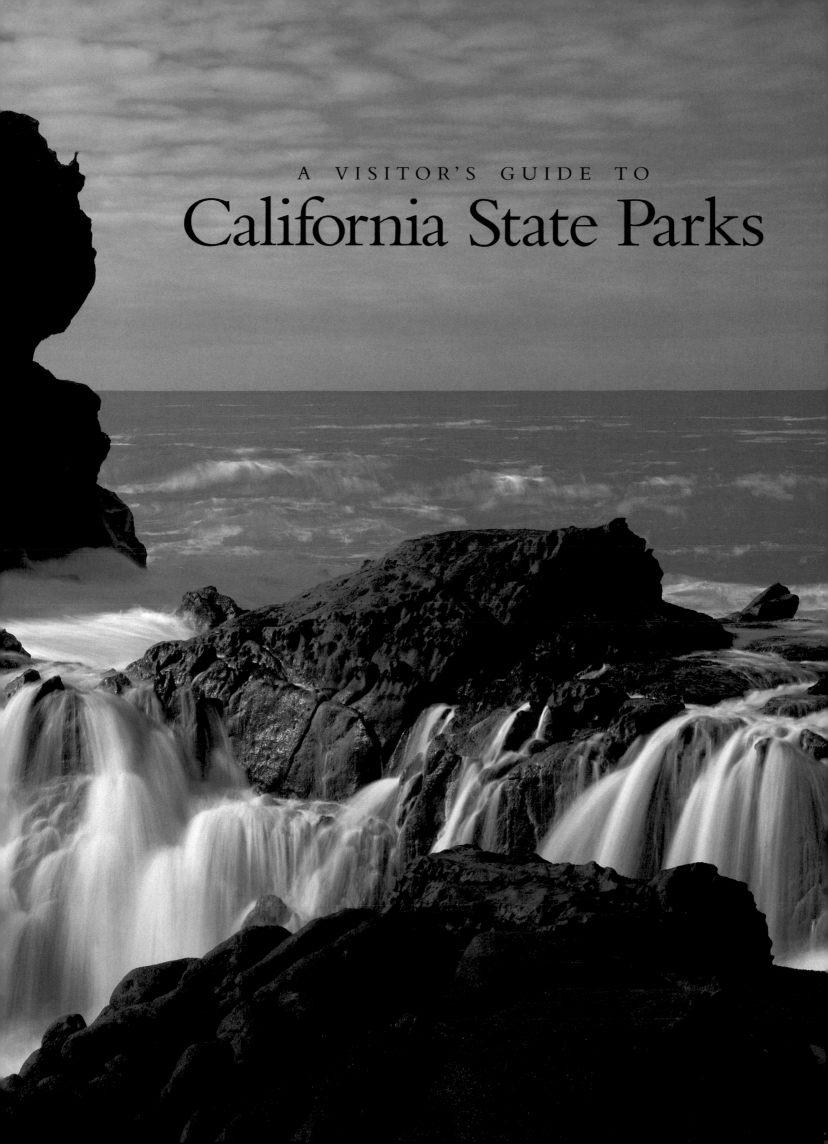

A VISITOR'S GUIDE TO
California State Parks

State of California • The Resources Agency

Department of Parks & Recreation

P.O. Box 2390 • Sacramento, California 95811

SEQUOIA
COMMUNICATIONS

Produced by Sequoia Communications
2020 Alameda Padre Serra, Suite 220, Santa Barbara, CA 93103
(805) 963-9336

Authors: Walter Houk *(Southern California),* Sue Irwin *(Central
California),* Richard A. Lovett *(Northern California)*

Managing Editor for State of California
Department of Parks and Recreation:
Joseph H. Engbeck, Jr.
Editors: John Evarts, Nicky Leach, Lynn Purl,
and Lucinda Ronyecz
Contributing Editors: Jill Canon, John Evarts, Marie Hathaway
Editorial Assistants: Don Dennis, DeLynn Garner-Kelley,
Gilda Parodi-Swords, and Jackie Terry
Design: Adine Maron
Design and Production Assistants:
Brooks Branch and Karen Hubbard
Typesetting: Graphic Traffic

Library of Congress No. 89-063125
ISBN: 0-941925-05-6

Printed in Hong Kong
First printing, 1990

Photography

FRANK S. BALTHIS: 12 (top); 14 (bottom); 16; 23; 32 (bottom); 38 (top right); 42 (right); 46 (bottom & middle); 48 (bottom); 56 (bottom); 73; 80; 115; 117; 118. TOM BEAN: 14 (top). WILLARD CLAY: 24; 33; 36 (top); 56-57; 88. RALPH CLEVENGER: Front cover flap; 46 (top); 56 (top) 89; 100 (bottom & top); 106 (bottom & top). CARR CLIFTON: Inside front cover 2-3; 8-9; 21 (top); 44; 55 (top); 60(top); 67 (bottom); 71 (top); 76; 101 (bottom); 109 (top) 111 (top); 112-113. ED COOPER: 13 (top); 18-19; 25; 42-43; 47; 67 (top); 101 (top). BILL EVARTS: 26 (bottom); 30 (center); 62-63; 68 (top & top right); 94 (top); 96 (bottom); 98; 99; 100 (middle); 104; 105; 106-107; 108 (left); 109 (bottom); 111 (bottom); 112 (left). JOHN EVARTS: 108 (right). RUSS FINLEY: 70-71. CHARLES GARDNER: 81; 82 (bottom & top); 86 (bottom & top); 90 (bottom). FREDERICA GEORGIA: 26 (top); 34; 41; 42 (left). DANIEL GOTSHALL: 54 (bottom). TONY HERTZ: 15. JUSTINE HILL: 26-27; 37 (bottom); 85 (bottom); 87; 90 (top); 93 (top); 102 (right); 112 (right). FRED HIRSCHMANN: 45; 50; 62 (top). PHILIP HYDE: 28. SUE IRWIN: 52 (top). PAUL JOHNSON: 60 (bottom); 92. LEWIS KEMPER: 22 (top). CHARLES KENNARD: 11, 12(center); 17 (bottom); 30 (top); 38 (bottom); 48 (top). ROBERT LATSON: 31 (top); 59 (top). J.C. LEACOCK: Back flap. PAUL LEIB: 84 (top left). RICK LOVETT: 22 (bottom); 31 (bottom); 39; 102 (left); 116. GARY MOON: 18 (bottom inset); 20; 30 (bottom); 32 (top). CARA MOORE: 52 (bottom); 55 (bottom); 59 (bottom); 61; 66(middle); 72; 75; 77; 78 (bottom & top); 82 (middle); 85 (top). ROBERT MORRIS: 53; 54 (top); 83 (bottom & top); 84 (bottom); 94 (bottom); 97; 103; 119. TOM MYERS: 17 (top); 29; 36-37; 36 (bottom inset); 38 (top left); 40; 66 (top); 71 (bottom); 94-95; 95 (inset). PAT O'HARA: Back cover; 27; 64; 76-77; 96 (top) 110. ROBERT PARKER: 51; 74 (right); 79. LARRY ULRICH: Front cover; 6; 10; 13 (bottom); 18 (top, inset); 21 (bottom); 35; 58; 68 (bottom); 69; 74 (left); 88-89; 91; 93 (bottom). KENNAN WARD: 12 (bottom); 49; 62 (bottom). DAVID WYMAN: 66 (bottom).

(Title pages): Rocky surfline, Salt Point State Park.

Terry Parker

OFFICE OF THE GOVERNOR
State of California

August 17, 1989

It is my great pleasure to invite you to enjoy the natural beauty and many recreational opportunities available throughout the California State Park System. This magnificent system is one of endless diversity, offering recreation, habitat and wildlife protection, and preservation of historic buildings and landmarks throughout our great state. The beaches, rivers, lakes, mountains, forests, valleys and historical sites that are preserved and made accessible by the California State Park System help make the Golden State attractive to business while supporting our state's strong tourism industry.

The quality and success of California's State Park System flow directly from the many groups and individuals who have dedicated their time, energy and expertise to its development, maintenance and progress. This unique system did not originate through governmental channels, but was the dream of private citizens who had the wisdom to recognize the vital need for wildlife and habitat protection and historic site preservation. Through their efforts, and the dedicated and concerned supervision of park professionals, California's state parks have earned a lasting reputation as some of the finest in the nation.

This book clearly details the spectacular beauty of our state parks and provides an insight into the effective preservation and maintenance programs offered by the California State Park System and many public and private organizations. California truly has something to offer for everyone, and I hope this publication will encourage you to explore and discover the wonders and beauty of the California State Park System.

Most cordially,

George Deukmejian

George Deukmejian

Acknowledgements

An extraordinary number of people have participated in the compilation and review of the material that appears in this book. Those who read the manuscript as a whole or in large part and provided helpful commentary at various points along the way include Dorene Clement, Rodi Fregien, Bud Getty, Jim Woodward (and his son David). Those who reviewed the basic concept or working outline of the book, reviewed parts of the manuscript, or coordinated review by others include Bill Berry, Kathy Franklin, Dom Gotelli, Don Ito, Bruce Kennedy, Vic Maris, Dick McKillop, Patty Posner, Donna Pozzi, Carrie Salisbury, Sally Scott, Al Ulm, and Denzil Verardo. John Evarts, Nicky Leach, Adine Maron, and Lucinda Ronyecz led the effort for Sequoia Communications. But, of course, a book like this could not be produced without help from those dedicated and generous people, far too numerous to list, who took time from their busy schedules to provide basic information to the writers and editors of this project from the very beginning. Your help is greatly appreciated!

—Joseph H. Engbeck, Jr.
California State Department of Parks and Recreation

Table of Contents

Western rhododendron and coast redwoods, Kruse
Rhododendron State Reserve, Sonoma County.

Visiting California's State Parks

Native fan palms, Anza-Borrego Desert State Park.

Recreational opportunities abound in the nearly 300 parks that make up the California State Park System. Summer is the most popular time to visit most parks, though it is also the most difficult time to get a campsite reservation. Annual attendance amounts to some 73 million visitors—mostly in the summer.

But California's world-renowned climate makes it possible to enjoy the outdoors from early spring until the rains of early autumn. And even winter has its possibilities: Cross-country skiing in the Sierra Nevada; sunbathing in the Southern California desert; cool-weather trips to California's spectacular, thousand-mile-long coastline; or a trip into the past in a state historic park or museum.

The California State Park System has classified its park units to provide maximum recreational opportunity consistent with protecting scenic, scientific, natural, or historical values. **State parks** contain outstanding scenic, natural, cultural, or ecological values. **State wildernesses** feature an undeveloped area's natural, primeval character. **State reserves** have outstanding or unusual natural or scenic values. **State historic units** preserve places and objects of statewide historic significance. Several classes are devoted to recreation: **state recreation areas, beaches, state vehicular recreation areas,** and **wayside campgrounds.** Any park unit may include a **natural preserve**—an area of natural or scientific significance sometimes containing rare or endangered plant species, or unique geological or topographical features.

The range of activities in California's state parks is almost endless. In addition to many special events, there are regularly scheduled nature hikes, campfire programs, Junior Ranger programs, and interpretive talks at most state parks. Special arrangements can also be made for rangers to speak to school children and community organizations.

Facilities are available in many state parks for special activities such as weddings, meetings, or conventions. Some group campgrounds can accommodate large numbers of people. Check the Group Camping list at the end of this book or call the park for more information.

Some state parks, especially historic parks and museums, are closed on Thanksgiving, Christmas, and New Year's Day. For more specific information, call the park you are interested in visiting.

A more complete listing of state park special events for the current year is available from: California Department of Parks and Recreation, Special Events Calendar, Office of Public Relations, tions, P.O. Box 942896, Sacramento, CA 94296-0001. Tel: (916) 445-6477.

Camping is very popular in the State Park System. Campgrounds are given the following designations: **Developed:** Ordinarily has improved roads, restrooms (with hot showers, unless otherwise indicated), piped drinking water, and campsites with table, stove, or fire ring. **Primitive:** Typically has chemical or pit toilets, tables, and a central water supply. Some have no facilities. **Trailer Hookups:** Available in only a few parks (see listing in back). Trailers, campers, and motorhomes may also use developed or primitive campsites. Reservations are advisable for campers with large vehicles since only a few sites in each park may be

able to accommodate the maximum size. **Enroute:** Day-use parking areas that can be used by self-contained trailers, campers, or motorhomes on an overnight basis. Campsites must be vacated by 9 a.m. **Environmental:** Primitive sites in relatively undisturbed natural settings. A short walk is required to reach these relatively isolated campsites. Be prepared to carry in water and other supplies. (See sidebar on page 27 in book.)

Most family, group, and environmental campsites and cabins can be reserved in advance through MISTIX. Reservations are recommended for summer and holiday visits. You can reserve campsites up to eight weeks in advance, or as late as the day before the date of reservation. The official camping day begins and ends at 2 p.m. You may be able to occupy the campsite early if it is vacant, but you must check out before 2 p.m. on your last day.

To make reservations, call MISTIX at 1-800-444-PARK and use your VISA or MasterCard. If you are calling from out of state, the number to use is (619) 452-1950. For mail-in reservations, write to MISTIX, P.O. Box 85705, San Diego, CA 92138-5705. Payment must be received at least seven days in advance of the reservation date. The hearing impaired can call the MISTIX TDD number, 1-800-274-PARK. The same telephone numbers can also be used to reserve tours at Hearst Castle or to reserve group camp or group picnic areas.

Annual passes are available for frequent users of state park day-use facilities, including boat launching. Passes allow an unlimited number of entries during the calendar year, provided the park is open and space is available. The **Golden Bear Pass** is for people who are 62 years or older with limited incomes. Those receiving aid to the blind, disabled, or Aid to Families with Dependent Children through the Department of Social Services are eligible. A **Disabled Veteran's Pass** is also available. For further information about prices, privileges, and any restrictions that may apply, contact the Department of Parks and Recreation, Office of Public Relations, at the previously mentioned address.

CHAPTER ONE

Northern California Coast

California's north coast country is a land of contrast and mystery, of fog-shrouded redwoods and crashing, storm-tossed surf, of sun-drenched coastal valleys and sandy beaches. It contains California's only completely wild river, the Smith, and countless opportunities for fishing and other water-oriented recreation. In the southern part of this territory there are over a dozen state parks—easily reached from the San Francisco Bay Area—that showcase the rich cultural and natural history of the region.

In the far north Del Norte and Humboldt counties enjoy a combination of summer fog and heavy winter rain that makes it possible for a magnificent forest of coast redwoods to prosper. Several state redwood parks are located near U.S. Highway 101 along the coastal shelf between the sea and the 6,000-foot-high peaks of the Klamath Range. Visitors come to camp and hike among the redwoods at Prairie Creek, Jedediah Smith, and Del Norte Coast state parks. Along the coast are a number of state beaches, where rocky headlands, dunes, and secluded stretches of sand can be explored. In Eureka, the North Coast's largest city, a logging museum and an Indian museum are open to visitors at Fort Humboldt State Historic Park.

South of Eureka, Highway 101 turns inland, and passes through or very close to a whole string of redwood parks along the South Fork of the Eel River. Humboldt Redwoods State Park includes perhaps the most impressive grove of primeval redwoods to be found anywhere, and a variety of other parks offer attractions that range from wilderness hiking to car camping alongside grassy meadows overlooking the sea.

South of the Eel River, the mountains of the Coast Range become lower and recede somewhat from the ocean, leaving a coastline of fissured bluffs and grassy headlands centering around the town of Mendocino. This area is especially popular with abalone divers, hikers, and nature lovers. Within a stretch of coast that is no more than 20 miles long, seven separate parks provide an extrordinary range of recreational opportunities.

South of Mendocino, the coast is relatively open, the bluffs are lower, and fine beaches such as the ones at Manchester or Sonoma Coast occur more and more often. Scattered groves of redwoods are preserved in some of the inland parks such as Samuel P. Taylor and Armstrong Redwoods, while in the northern San Francisco Bay area, Mount Tamalpais and Angel Island offer fine hiking opportunities within sight of the San Francisco skyline.

Inland from the coast, in a region centering around the famous wine districts of Napa and Sonoma counties, history, hiking, and camping dominate the scene, with sites such as Benicia Capitol and Sonoma state historic parks preserving important pieces of early California history, while nearby Annadel, Sugarloaf Ridge, and Robert Louis Stevenson state parks provide opportunities to explore the rugged hills of the Coast Range. For car campers, Bothe-Napa makes an excellent base for exploring Napa County, while Clear Lake State Park features campgrounds and boat-launching facilities on 19-mile-long Clear Lake, the largest natural lake entirely inside the boundaries of California.

(Above): Indian paintbrush at Jughandle State Reserve. (Opposite): Pink seathrift and boulders at sunset, Salt Point State Park.

(Clockwise from bottom): A family of elk at Prairie Creek State Park; Wooly bear caterpillar on purple lupine; Steller's jays at Prairie Creek Redwoods State Park.

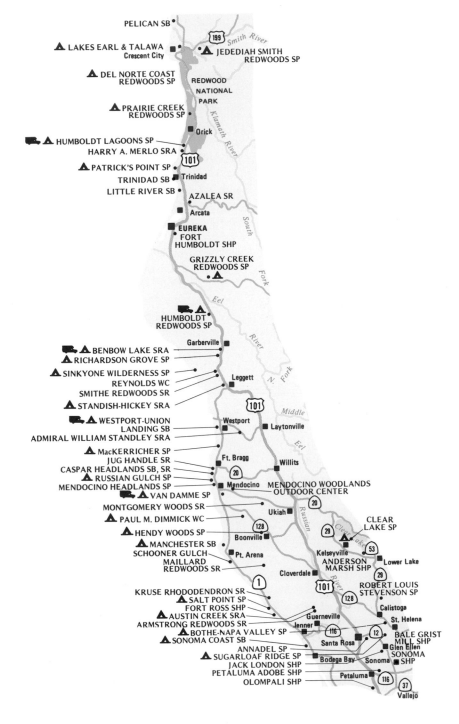

PELICAN SB •

▲ LAKES EARL & TALAWA
Crescent City

▲ JEDEDIAH SMITH
REDWOODS SP

199 Smith River

▲ DEL NORTE COAST
REDWOODS SP

REDWOOD
NATIONAL
PARK

▲ PRAIRIE CREEK
REDWOODS SP

Orick

Klamath River

🚐 ▲ HUMBOLDT LAGOONS SP

HARRY A. MERLO SRA

101

▲ PATRICK'S POINT SP

TRINIDAD SB • Trinidad

LITTLE RIVER SB •

AZALEA SR

South

■ Arcata

■ EUREKA
FORT
HUMBOLDT SHP

GRIZZLY CREEK
REDWOODS SP
• ▲

Fork

Eel

🚐 ▲
HUMBOLDT
REDWOODS SP

River

🚐 ▲ BENBOW LAKE SRA

Garberville ■

▲ RICHARDSON GROVE SP

▲ SINKYONE WILDERNESS SP

REYNOLDS WC

SMITHE REDWOODS SR

N. Fork

Leggett

▲ STANDISH-HICKEY SRA

101

Middle

🚐 ▲ WESTPORT-UNION
LANDING SB

ADMIRAL WILLIAM STANDLEY SRA

Westport

■ Laytonville

Eel

▲ MacKERRICHER SP

JUG HANDLE SR

CASPAR HEADLANDS SB, SR

▲ RUSSIAN GULCH SP

MENDOCINO HEADLANDS SP

Ft. Bragg

■ Willits

20

🚐 ▲ VAN DAMME SP

Mendocino

MENDOCINO WOODLANDS
OUTDOOR CENTER

MONTGOMERY WOODS SR

20

▲ PAUL M. DIMMICK WC

Ukiah

Russian

CLEAR
LAKE SP

▲ HENDY WOODS SP

128

29

▲

Boonville

▲ MANCHESTER SB

53

SCHOONER GULCH

Pt. Arena

Kelseyville

ANDERSON
MARSH SHP

Lower Lake

MAILLARD
REDWOODS SR

Cloverdale

29

KRUSE RHODODENDRON SR

1

101

128

ROBERT LOUIS
STEVENSON SP

▲ SALT POINT SP

FORT ROSS SHP

Calistoga

▲ AUSTIN CREEK SRA

ARMSTRONG REDWOODS SR

Guerneville

Jenner

St. Helena

▲ BOTHE-NAPA VALLEY SP

116

12

BALE GRIST
MILL SHP

▲ SONOMA COAST SB

Santa Rosa

Glen Ellen

ANNADEL SP

SONOMA
SHP

▲ SUGARLOAF RIDGE SP

Bodega Bay

Sonoma

JACK LONDON SHP

PETALUMA ADOBE SHP

Petaluma

116

OLOMPALI SHP

37

Vallejo

Humboldt and Del Norte Counties

Pelican State Beach

Pelican State Beach has the distinction of being the northernmost unit in the state park system. Located only a few yards from the Oregon border, it consists of a small, secluded beach that is an excellent place for walking and beachcombing. The beach is 21 miles north of Crescent City, off U.S. Highway 101. Access is via the last road before the agricultural inspection station. Look for the Pelican Beach Motel on the other side of the highway. After leaving the highway, bear right at the first opportunity. (707) 464-9533 or 458-3310.

Lakes Earl and Talawa

At the mouth of the Smith River lies a large delta consisting of miles of sandy beach, grass-covered dunes, twisted pines, and a system of lakes, ponds, mud flats, and marshes that support a diversity of fish and wildlife. Part of the area is under the jurisdiction of the California Department of Fish and Game; much of the rest lies within the 5,000-acre park unit known as Lakes Earl and Talawa. Presently developed only for low-intensity uses, the area features opportunities for fishing either in the river, the ocean, or the brackish lakes; king salmon, silver salmon, cutthroat trout, and steelhead are found here. Other popular activities are hiking, horseback riding, bird watching, boating, and waterfowl hunting. Environ-

mental campsites are available as well. There are several access routes, which unfortunately are all poorly marked. The simplest route is to take Lake Earl Dr. (Northcrest Dr. at its southern end), which parallels U.S. Highway 101 on the ocean side between Crescent City and the mouth of the Smith River. Look for signs designating beach or coastal access. (707) 464-9533.

Jedediah Smith Redwoods State Park

In 1826 Jedediah Smith became the first American to travel overland from the Mississippi River to California, and in 1827 was the first white person to cross the Sierra Nevada. A man of extrordinary ability with an amazing instinct for survival, Smith left his mark not only on the map of California but also in the hearts of many who knew him, and many more who have read about him over the years. It is fitting that one of the finest redwood groves in the state park system stands in the park named for him. But redwoods are not the most unusual feature of this 9,500-acre park. Rather, it is the Smith River itself, also named for him, which is now the last major river in California without a dam. Draining a relatively undisturbed watershed, it holds the state record for steelhead (over 27 pounds), and even after a major storm, it is fishable again within two or three days.

The park contains 18 miles of hiking trails, 108 developed campsites, several groves of old-growth redwoods. One

grove covers 5,000 acres and includes one of the world's largest (not tallest) coast redwoods—a tree that measures 20 feet in diameter and 340 feet in height. Located on Highway 199, the park is nine miles east of Crescent City. (707) 458-3310 or 464-9533.

Del Norte Coast Redwoods State Park

Del Norte Coast Redwoods State Park is best known for its unique combination of very dense old-growth redwoods and its spectacularly senic coastline. Some wonderful trails wander through the forest and down to the sea, including the exceptionally interesting Damnation Creek Trail. Wildlife within the park, including the marine life that can be observed along the shore and a wide variety of plant life typical of the redwood forest region combine to make this 6,400 acre park exceptionally enjoyable. A handsome 145-site campground nestles in a grove of second-growth redwoods with a thick understory of ferns and other native plants. The park is located seven miles south of Crescent City on U.S. Highway 101. (707) 445-6547 or 464-9533.

(Top left): Redwoods stand guard at Jedediah Smith State Park. (Above): Shrouded in mist, rhododendrons bring vivid color to the forest floor.

Prairie Creek Redwoods State Park

In Prairie Creek Redwoods State Park you can walk all day through a redwood forest for almost an entire day, or hike up a narrow, flat-bottomed canyon whose vertical 50-foot bluffs, crowned by redwoods, are festooned with a dense growth of feathery ferns. Prairie Creek, the most diverse of the northern redwood parks, has 70 miles of hiking trails, 100 developed campsites, a long beach at the ocean, and herds of Roosevelt elk, some of which are usually visible from the highway near the visitor center. Special features of the park include two designated jogging trails totaling seven miles, 20 miles of trail open to mountain bikes, and a ⅓-mile nature trail for blind or disabled visitors (tape players are available in the visitor center). Fishermen enjoy surf fishing for red-tailed perch, or netting smelt along the beach. Prairie Creek is located along eight miles of U.S. Highway 101, fifty miles north of Eureka. (707) 488-2171.

Humboldt Lagoons State Park/ Harry A. Merlo State Recreation Area

Three lagoons are contained in Humboldt Lagoons State Park and adjacent Harry A. Merlo State Recreation Area. Two of them—Stone Lagoon and Big Lagoon—display a fascinating, periodic cycle. Upon filling with water during heavy storm seasons they overflow, and the resulting exit stream carves a channel that can drop the lagoon's water level by as much as 6 feet in a single hour. Once the lagoon has drained, however, the actions of surf and tide repair the breach, and within a few days or weeks, it begins to fill again. The third lagoon—somewhat inappro-

priately named Dry Lagoon—has been transformed into a freshwater marsh which no longer breaches into the ocean.

With their mixtures of salt and fresh water, the lagoons at these parks are excellent sites for fishing, boating, bird watching, and windsurfing; park visitors also enjoy a stroll on the driftwood-strewn beach. There is no camping at Harry A. Merlo, but Humboldt Lagoons has a 25-site primitive campground (no water), as well as boat-in and walk-in environmental campsites. The two parks are located 32 miles north of Eureka on U.S. Highway 101. (707) 488-2171.

Patrick's Point State Park

Patrick's Point State Park, situated on a headland jutting out into the Pacific, is an ideal place to explore a pristine stretch of North Coast shoreline. A broad two-mile beach runs north from the state park, where beachcombers can hunt for agates polished by the waves, while high bluffs within the park provide excellent sites for whale-watching or for simply contemplating the crash of waves on offshore rocks. This compact 632-acre park also has tide pools, a two-mile hiking trail along the bluffs, and 123 developed campsites. Look for sea lions and seals near the rocks at the southern end of the park. Located ½-mile west of U.S. Highway 101, Patrick's Point is 25 miles north of Eureka (five miles north of Trinidad). (707) 667-3570.

Trinidad State Beach

Nestled in a cove with a beach of fine dark sand, and framed by crashing surf and picturesque rocks, Trinidad is one of the loveliest beaches in Northern California. Although it isn't very big—you can walk its entire length in a few minutes—it is a fascinating stretch of coast to visit, particularly when low tide has widened it to its maximum extent. The trail down to the beach makes an excellent nature hike, passing through woods and across open bluffs that are strewn with wildflowers in late spring. Look also for the natural arch at the north end of the beach. A pleasant picnic area and the parking lot are atop the bluffs. To get there, exit U.S. Highway 101 at Trinidad, heading toward

the coast until you see signs for the beach. There is no camping. (707) 677-3570 or 445-6547.

Little River State Beach

Little River State Beach is a broad expanse of smooth sand and low dunes at the mouth of Little River. Presently undeveloped, the park consists of 112 acres on the south side of the river, but the adjacent beach continues southward for several miles. There are no facilities, not even a parking lot, but Humboldt County's Clam Beach Park adjoining it to the south provides a variety of facilities, including camping. To get there, exit U.S. Highway 101 at the south end of the Little River bridge, five miles south of Trinidad (13 miles north of Eureka). (707) 677-3570 or 445-6547.

Azalea State Reserve

Azalea State Reserve is one of the few parks in which nature has not been allowed to run its course. The reason is simple: the western azalea thrives best in open areas, but open hillsides on the North Coast quickly turn to forest. So, for the sake of the azaleas in this 30-acre reserve, the timber has been removed and the shrubs allowed to flourish in grand profusion. At peak blooming season in May and June, the azaleas put on a stunning display of massed pink and white flowers, with the heady perfume of thousands of blossoms filling the air. The reserve is located on Highway 200, which cuts the corner between U.S. Highway 199 and U.S. Highway 101, north of the Mad River. Look for exit signs marked North Bank Rd. The turn-off from Highway 200 is marked. (707) 677-3570 or 443-4588.

(Top left): Prairie Creek State Park. (Above): Azaleas at Stage Coach Hill, Azalea State Reserve.

Fort Humboldt State Historic Park

Dispatched to protect early settlers in the remote Humboldt Bay region, Brevet Lt. Colonel Robert C. Buchanan and a group of soldiers established a 14-building outpost on an exposed bluff overlooking the bay in 1854. Today, the park preserves the ruins of Fort Humboldt, including the fort's hospital and a reconstruction of the surgeon's quarters. The hospital now contains a museum that depicts the traditional Indian way of life here, and recounts the tragic violence that flared as gold miners and other settlers encroached on Indian hunting and fishing grounds between the early 1850s and 1866.

Fort Humboldt State Historic Park also contains a series of exhibits in its outdoor logging display (wheelchair accessible), which shows the techniques used in the early days of the lumber industry when trees were cut by hand and hauled away by ox teams or by steam engines known as "steam donkeys." On the third Saturday of every month during the summer, the park holds a "steam-up," when it fires up some of the donkeys and one or more steam locomotives. Once a year, in late April, a logging competition accompanies the steam-up. Fort Humboldt is located on Highland Ave., which intersects U.S. Highway 101 on the south side of Eureka. (707) 445-6567 or 445-6547.

Grizzly Creek Redwoods State Park

Although Grizzly Creek Redwoods State Park covers only a few acres, it is large enough to provide a sense of seclusion, and it receives so few visitors that on a weekday it is possible to be the only person in one of its groves of coast redwoods. Located where Grizzly Creek meets the Van Duzen River, this lush, green, 390-acre park is a pleasant place for a vacation off the beaten track. A small (30-unit) campground includes drinking water, stoves, picnic tables, and cupboards. There are six short hiking trails, two of which are only accessible in summer when low water permits installation of a temporary bridge across the river. Fishing and swimming are popular, and there is a 30-unit picnic area for day use. Overnight visitors should be aware, however, that the campground lies very close to the high-

Portions of the original 1854 military outpost are preserved at Fort Humboldt State Historic Park.

way. The park is located on Highway 36, 18 miles east of U.S. Highway 101. Vehicles pulling trailers should not approach from the east. (707) 777-3683 or 946-2311.

Humboldt Redwoods State Park

Many vacationers, hurrying along U.S. Highway 101 to other destinations, unknowingly pass right by the single most impressive stand of redwoods to be found anywhere in the world. Located in 51,000-acre Humboldt Redwoods State Park and known as the Rockefeller Forest, this stand of trees contains approximately 10,000 acres of old-growth redwoods—nearly ⅛ of California's remaining old-growth redwoods. A five-mile-long road winds through this grove, while more than 100 miles of hiking trails make it easy to explore not only this matchless grove, but also an additional 8,000 acres of old-growth redwoods and the whole watershed of Bull Creek. The park also contains the Dyerville Giant, one of the largest and tallest coast redwoods.

Along with strolling, hiking, and nature studies, popular activities include horseback riding, mountain biking (fire roads only), and fishing and swimming in the South Fork of the Eel River. Due to fire danger, camping is allowed only in designated areas. Along with 247 developed family sites, there is a hike-and-bike camp, a primitive camp which can accommodate up to 50

equestrians, and a group camp. The spectacularly scenic Avenue of the Giants Parkway runs through the park parallel to U.S. Highway 101. Each spring this unique 33-mile-long parkway draws runners from all over the state to compete in an annual marathon. The park lies on both sides of U.S. Highway 101, 45 miles south of Eureka, near Weott. (707) 946-2311.

Benbow Lake State Recreation Area

Tiny Benbow Lake is a beginning canoeist's delight. Motorboats are prohibited on this lake, which occupies about a mile of the South Fork of the Eel River and is fully contained in 780-acre Benbow Lake State Recreation Area. A concessionaire rents canoes and paddleboats, and several times a week park staff lead "canoe hikes" to explore the lake shore. The park also has three miles of trails, a 76-site developed campground (closed November 1 to March 31), a Shakespeare festival, and a summer arts festival. It also has swimming and fishing. The lake itself is only seasonal; the dam is put in place in May and removed in September. Benbow Lake is located two miles south of Garberville off U.S. Highway 101. (707) 946-2311.

Richardson Grove State Park

Affectionately known as "The Grove" by regular visitors, Richardson Grove is one of the oldest state parks, dating back to the early 1920s when it was acquired and named after Governor William Friend Richardson. In addition to the grove itself, primary attractions include 169 developed campsites, a visitor center built from an old lodge, a walk-through tree, a thriving dawn redwood imported from China, and interpretive programs and displays describing the natural history of the area. Visitors to the 1,000-acre park can also hike, fish for steelhead and trout during the rainy season, or visit swimming holes and river beaches, which on warm summer days one local resident has nicknamed the "Little Riviera." The park is located on the South Fork of the Eel River, eight miles south of Garberville on U.S. Highway 101. (707) 247-3318 or 946-2311.

Standish-Hickey State Recreation Area

Smaller, less heavily visited, and somewhat more personal than the larger and more famous redwood parks to the north, Standish-Hickey is a place that many people return to year after year, generation after generation. Occupying both banks of the steep defile of the South Fork of the Eel River, the 1,020-acre park has three medium-sized campgrounds with a total of 162 developed sites, a good swimming hole, and fishing for steelhead and salmon during the fall and winter runs. Nine miles of hiking trails cover an elevation range between 800 and 1,600

feet and lead to several small groves of old-growth redwoods, one of which includes the 225-foot-high Miles Standish Tree. Standish-Hickey State Recreation Area is located one mile north of Leggett on U.S. Highway 101. (707) 925-6482 or 946-2311.

Westport-Union Landing State Beach

Westport-Union Landing State Beach features camp sites atop a grassy bluff with the waters of the Pacific lapping practically at their doorstep, 50 feet below. Surf fishermen enjoy the park's rock-studded beaches, while non-fishermen can explore tide pools or simply sit in camp and enjoy the sunset. Other popular activities include smelt fishing, abalone diving, and spear fishing. Winter surf can send sea spray splashing as high as the campgrounds, delighting visitors who marvel at the dramatic display of wind and waves. There are seven campgrounds offering a total of 130 primitive sites along nearly two miles of coastal bluffs. The state beach is located two miles north of Westport off Highway 1. (707) 937-5804.

Admiral William Standley State Recreation Area

Admiral William Standley State Recreation Area is a park for people who like to explore back roads. So isolated that it receives only a few visitors, it consists of a 45-acre redwood grove situated at

1,700 feet in the Coast Range. With no developed facilities, picnicking and hiking are the primary recreational activities here. The park is 14 miles west of Laytonville on Branscomb Rd. The road continues to the coast, but much of it is unpaved. (707) 946-2311.

MacKerricher State Beach

MacKerricher State Beach includes some eight miles of beach, gentle lowlands, and several square miles of sand dunes that provide a pleasant contrast to the characteristically rugged shoreline of the North Coast. A park for hikers, joggers, bicyclists, fishermen, and nature lovers, it offers two freshwater lakes (one of which is stocked with trout) a wheelchair-accessible nature trail, and seven miles of abandoned (but still paved) road most of which is open only to foot traffic, bicycles, and horses. One of the most popular areas of the park is Laguna Point (also wheelchair accessible) where there is a resident population of harbor seals. During the winter and spring months the nearby headland also makes a good lookout for whale watching from about November to March. Ranger-led nature hikes are scheduled periodically and include whale watching from about November to March. The 1,600-acre park also has 143 developed campsites, plus 11 walk-in sites that are easily accessible but nevertheless offer a camping experience similar to a short-distance backpack. The park is located on the outskirts of Cleone, three miles north of Fort Bragg on Highway 1. (707) 937-5804.

Mendocino County

Sinkyone Wilderness State Park

Several California state parks have designated wilderness areas within their boundaries, but only 7,000-acre Sinkyone Wilderness State Park carries the word "wilderness" in its name. Located on a section of coast popularly known as the "lost coast," it occupies one of the few lengthy portions of California coast not accessible by highway. Even today, access is possible only over steep, narrow gravel roads, and the country has changed very little since the days when the Sinkyone Indians were the

only human residents of this area. Sinkyone is a land of forests, prairies, bluffs, beaches, and tidepools. It also has three small groves of old-growth redwoods and a herd of Roosevelt elk introduced from Prairie Creek State Park to replace those that had been exterminated in the 19th century.

As its name suggests, Sinkyone Wilderness is predominantly a hiker's and backpacker's park, with the 17-mile Lost Coast Trail running its entire length. Due to rugged terrain, backpackers should allow three days for a one-way trek on this trail; overnight permits are required. There is a primitive 15-site drive-in campground at the park's southern entrance and a walk-in campground just 75 yards from the parking area at the northern entrance. Day hiking is best from the north, where easier terrain allows longer excursions. Access to the south end of the park is via a gravel road (County Rd. 431) which leaves Highway 1 at milepost 90.88 between Leggett and the coast; for access to the northern part of the park follow Briceland Thorne Rd. (County Rd. 435) for 30 miles west from Redway. A good road map of the region is recommended. (707) 946-2311.

Reynolds Wayside Campground
This park is named for Frank W. Reynolds, an early conservationist whose efforts helped bring about the the Forest Practices Act of 1939—landmark legislation which first placed controls on the size of trees to be cut, the number of seed trees to be left, and the clean-up of logging debris. Reynolds Wayside Campground was originally a 407-acre resort run by the Reynolds family, situated on a bluff overlooking the South Fork of the Eel River. The area was acquired in 1965 for state park purposes, though a freeway was built through part of the property a few years later. Since then, land exchanges for acreage in Sinkyone Wilderness have further reduced the park to one small stand of old-growth trees on 68 acres, with access to the river below. The park is reached by exiting U.S. Highway 101 at milepost 99.5 (marked as Highway 271). The unmarked park entrance lies just west of the freeway on an overgrown road with a steel gate. (707) 946-2311.

Smithe Redwoods State Reserve
The centerpiece of Smithe Redwoods is the Frank and Bess Smithe Grove, a small grove of redwoods that until the 1960s was a private resort, with cabins, a restaurant, and a store. Typical of commercial development in the redwoods, the restaurant was entered through two walk-through trees, with a third redwood growing through the roof. In addition to the redwoods, the 620-acre park has picnic areas, trails, and a 60-foot waterfall, with fishing and swimming in the South Fork of the Eel. It is located four miles north of Leggett on U.S. Highway 101. (707) 247-3318 or 946-2311.

Jughandle State Reserve
A hike up the ecological staircase—the principal attraction in Jughandle State Reserve—is a journey both backward and forward in time. It is a journey backward because as you hike the 2½-mile nature trail, you climb through a set of five low terraces, each of which was uplifted from sea level about 100,000 years before the one below it. It is a journey forward because the plants on each terrace represent a more advanced stage in succession, indicating what the previous, next lower terrace may look like 100,000 years from now.

Ecologically, each is fascinating. The lowest one consists of coastal prairie flanked by crashing surf, while the second is covered by pines. The third, however, is by far the most interesting. With its soil leached of nutrients by the heavy rainfall, and underlain by a layer

(Opposite): Visitor center lodge, Richardson Grove. (Top): Canoers on Lake Cleone, MacKerricher State Park. (Above): The dramatic Sinkyone Wilderness coastline.

of fused soil called "hardpan," it supports a unique pygmy forest in which knee-high trees may be several decades old. A self-guiding trail booklet explaining the ecological and geological features that culminate in this pygmy forest can be purchased at the trailhead. The 769-acre preserve straddles Highway 1, one mile north of Caspar. (707) 937-5804.

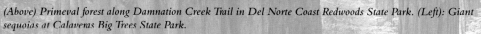
(Above) Primeval forest along Damnation Creek Trail in Del Norte Coast Redwoods State Park. (Left): Giant sequoias at Calaveras Big Trees State Park.

California's Redwoods:
The World's Tallest and Largest Living Things

Giant survivors from an age of giants." That is how one observer has described the redwoods of the California coast and their inland cousins, the sequoias. It is an accurate description. Not only do the massive boles of these trees dwarf any possible comparison, but they are living remnants from the age of dinosaurs when both plants and animals grew to mammoth proportions.

Millions of years ago, the ancestors of our present-day redwoods covered much of the northern hemisphere. The cold climate of the Ice Age reduced their range to a narrow belt along the California coast where heavy rainfall and persistent summer fog fulfill the trees' need for adequate year-round moisture. When the first Europeans arrived, the redwood belt covered some 2 million acres—a seemingly endless forest of giants. By the early 20th century, however, the lumber industry had already harvested substantial portions of this vast acreage and it was fast becoming apparent that unless something was done to protect them, primeval redwood forests would soon be a thing of the past.

The battle to preserve the redwoods ultimately led to the creation of the California State Park System, and with the help of the Save-the-Redwoods League, more than 50,000 acres of old-growth redwood forest have now been given permanent protection. State parks also include thousands of acres of second-growth redwoods—

younger trees, some of which are already sizeable, and which will someday be towering giants that can inspire and delight future generations. Big Basin Redwoods State Park, acquired in 1902, was the first to be included in the present California system. Prairie Creek, Humboldt Redwoods, and other North Coast redwood parks followed in the 1920s and 1930s. Today, there are more than 30 redwood parks scattered along 500 miles of California coast, ranging from near the Oregon border to Big Sur.

Within these parks there are trees that tower more than 350 feet above the ground—trees that may be 2,000 years old and as much as 20 feet in diameter. California's redwood parks are a national treasure, unique forests that beckon visitors from all over the world to stroll in their hushed, cathedral-like silence, to hike among lush ferns and delicate redwood sorrel on the forest floor, and to gaze awestruck at the size and grace of the redwoods themselves.

Each park has its own charm, but the very largest and most-impressive old-growth forests are found in North Coast parks such as Humboldt Redwoods, Prairie Creek, Jedediah Smith, and Del Norte Coast. Near San Francisco, the largest and most accessible redwood groves are in Big Basin, Armstrong Redwoods, Mount Tamalpais, and Samuel P. Taylor state parks.

California's other species of redwood, the big tree or giant sequoia, is found in isolated groves between

4,500 and 8,000 feet elevations on the western slope of the southern Sierra Nevada. Not so tall, but more massive than their coastal cousins, these trees are the largest living things on earth. In 1852, the discovery of the magnificent grove of giant sequoias that is now protected in Calaveras Big Trees State Park brought worldwide attention to these fabulous trees.

A school field trip at Russian Gulch State Park.

Caspar Headlands State Beach

This small park holds three acres of sand beach flanked by low bluffs at the head of a small bay. A privately operated campground is nearby. Caspar Headlands State Beach is located two miles north of Russian Gulch on the coast access road (Point Cabrillo Dr.). From the north, it is found one mile south of the turn off at milepost 54.71 on Highway 1. (707) 937-5804.

Caspar Headlands State Reserve

Caspar Headlands State Reserve is surrounded by a housing development near the town of Caspar, but contains within its compact three acres a small strip of rugged coastline—a tiny wonderland of fissures, foaming waves, sculpted rocks, and wildflowers. Access to the reserve can be arranged prior to your visit by obtaining an entry permit (free of charge) from the California State Park district office at Russian Gulch. (707) 937-5804.

Russian Gulch State Park

Most people go to Russian Gulch State Park in order to enjoy the seashore, or to see the "Punch Bowl," a large, collapsed sea cave that waves enter through a tunnel in one side; once inside the bowl, the waves slosh about its cauldron-like interior, accompanied by a delightful array of throaty echoes. But Russian Gulch State Park offers far more than just its scenic coastline. Extending inland like a crooked finger along a twisting valley, the 1,300-acre park also contains several miles of hiking trails, a 36-foot waterfall, a primitive horse camp, and a paved bicycle trail along a disused park road. A com-fortable 30-unit campground, flanked by pine-clad hillsides, is situated in the woods near the mouth of the gulch. A nearby parking lot, located in the shadow of the picturesque arch of the Highway 1 bridge, provides day-use access for skin diving and rock fishing. The park is located two miles north of the town of Mendocino on Highway 1. (707) 937-5804.

Mendocino Headlands State Park

The grass-covered headlands, crashing surf, and fissured bluffs for which the Mendocino Coast is justifiably famous are well-represented in Mendocino Headlands State Park. Wrapped around three sides of the village of Mendocino in a greenbelt that contributes to the town's picturesque charm, this day-use only park features hiking, whale watching, abalone diving, and picnicking. It even has a sizeable beach, with access from the mouth of the Big River south of town. The historic old Ford House overlooking the bay on the south side of town features exhibits about human and natural history of the Mendocino Coast. (707) 937-5804.

Mendocino Woodlands Outdoor Center

Mendocino Woodlands Outdoor Center is a retreat and conference center among the redwoods east of Mendocino. Built at a cost of $1 million by the WPA and CCC during the great depression of the 1930's, this area is now operated for the California Department of of Parks and Recreation by the non-profit Mendocino Woodlands Camp Association. Situated amid 720 acres of redwood forest in the rugged Coast Range, the Outdoor Center features handsome and well-equipped rustic dining and recreation halls, Cabins, tent cabins, and restrooms. Three separate camp areas can accommodate a combined total of 440 people. It is open year-round and is located nine miles inland from Highway 1 east of Mendocino. For information, write the Mendocino Woodlands Camp Association, P.O. Box 267, Mendocino, CA 95460. (707) 937-5755.

Van Damme State Park

Van Damme State Park has a sheltered, easily accessible beach and is perhaps the best known abalone diving location on the entire North Coast. The park also has 10 miles of trail along the fern-carpeted canyon of Little River, and its boundaries extend inland over four miles. A paved road (which makes an excellent jogging path) is open to bicyclists for approximately half of that distance. There are also two short nature trails; one leads to a small bog, the other—accessible by wheelchair—visits a pygmy forest similar to one found at nearby Jug Handle State Reserve. The 2,160-acre park contains 74 developed campsites and 10 environmental campsites. Van Damme State Park is on Highway 1, three miles south of Mendocino. (707) 937-5804.

Montgomery Woods State Reserve

Montgomery Woods is one of the more remote of California's 31 redwood state parks. Covering 1,140 acres in the heart of the Coast Range, it is a day-use only park, offering picnicking and a two-mile self-guiding nature trail that visits five small but impressive stands of old-growth redwood trees. The park is located near Orrs Springs, the popular hot springs resort, 11 miles northwest of Ukiah on Comptche Rd. (also called Orr Springs Rd.). The park is also accessible via the gravel road from the town of Comptche to the west. (707) 937-5804.

Navarro River and Paul M. Dimmick Wayside Campground

Twelve miles of frontage along the Navarro river and some 650 acres of redwood and mixed conifer forest on the north side of the river were added to this park unit in 1988. Half of the fair market value of this acquisition ($3 million) was a gift from the Save-the-Redwoods League, which holds a permanent conservation easement designed to protect senic and natural values on some 550 acres of forestland south of the river. The park is located right on Highway 128 and includes a small campground (28 primitive campsites) about eight miles from the coast. Popular activities here include fishing in the spring, fall, and winter, canoeing and kayaking in late spring, and swimming and sunbathing in summer. Numerous memorial groves along the north side of the river are open for

day use and feature informal trails. (707) 937-5804.

Hendy Woods State Park

For more than 18 years, the stump of a fallen redwood on land that is now part of Hendy Woods State Park was the home of a man known as the Boonville Hermit. Today the hermit is gone, but when you visit this gentle park of towering trees and sun-drenched meadows it takes little effort to see what attracted him to stake out a home in this scenic area of inland Mendocino County. Located in the middle of the increasingly popular Anderson Valley wine district, this 690-acre park is warmer and less foggy than redwood parks near the coast. It makes a pleasant base camp for visitors to the wine country, and its frontage along the Navarro River provides steelhead fishing in the fall, swimming in the summer, and canoeing and kayaking during the receding floodwaters of late winter or early spring. There are two campgrounds with a combined total of 92 developed campsites. A wheelchair-accessible nature trail leads into the heart of an 80-acre redwood grove, one of two old-growth stands in the park.

Hendy Woods State Park is located eight miles northwest of Boonville, ½ mile south of Highway 128 on Philo Greenwood Rd. (707) 937-5804.

Maillard Redwoods State Reserve

Maillards Redwoods State Reserve protects 242 acres of virgin and second-growth redwoods. There is one picnic table and a parking lot that can accomodate up to five vehicles. The park is located 3½ miles west of Highway 128 on Fish Rock Rd; the turn-off is about 17 miles northwest of Cloverdale. The road, which is gravel surfaced, continues to Highway 1 near Anchor Bay. (707) 937-5804.

Manchester State Beach

Sun drenched or windswept, depending on the season, Manchester State Beach covers 1,400 acres just at the place where the San Andreas fault runs out to sea. This park contains one of the best surf-fishing beaches in Mendocino County as well as two creeks that have salmon and steelhead in winter. Bird-watchers enjoy the park's wetlands, which provide winter habitat for whistling swans. Beachcombers appreciate its five miles of gentle, sandy beach that

(Top): Mendocino Headlands State Park at sunset.
(Above): Fern Canyon, Van Damme State Park.

stretch southward toward the Point Arena Lighthouse. Forty-eight primitive campsites snuggle among grassy dunes that are ablaze with wildflowers in the spring and early summer; the park's 10 environmental campsites provide more privacy. Manchester State Beach surrounds the town of Manchester on three sides, but the entrance is ½ mile north of town on Highway 1. (707) 937-5804.

Schooner Gulch

Occupying 70 acres of beach and precipitous headlands, Schooner Gulch is an undeveloped—and relatively little known—state park property that preserves this scenic spot along the Mendocino Coast. It offers a stunning perch for watching sunsets or merely for sitting in the grass as the rays of the afternoon sun glisten on the waters below. Beachcombing and surf fishing are also possible activities. Schooner Gulch is located five miles south of Point Arena at the north side of the bridge at milepost 11.25 on Highway 1. (707) 937-5804.

(Top): Driftwood lies strewn along a misty Manchester Beach. (Above): Bale Grist Mill on the edge of the Napa Valley dates from the 1840s.

Clear Lake Area

Clear Lake State Park

Clear Lake is the largest natural freshwater lake completely within the borders of the state (Lake Tahoe is larger, but is partly in Nevada). Clear Lake State Park is situated on the lake's south shore and includes a low promontory overlooking the water. The park's primary attraction is the lake itself, which is 19 miles long and provides ample opportunity to boat and fish for crappie, bluegill, and black bass. Visitors also enjoy swimming and waterskiing in summer.

Park facilities include 147 developed sites among four mid-sized campgrounds, a swimming beach, and a boat ramp. A self-guiding trail shows how the Pomo Indians, who lived here for centuries, utilized the area's resources to meet their daily needs. The trail passes through the site of what was once a Pomo Indian village. A charming new visitor center features natural history exhibits about both the local landscape and the lake itself, as well as the human history of this area. The 560-acre park is located 3½ miles northeast of Kelseyville on Soda Bay Rd. (707) 279-4293.

Anderson Marsh State Historic Park

Anderson Marsh State Historic Park contains some 870 acres of oak woodland, grass-covered hills, and tule marsh at the southeast end of Clear Lake. The rich natural resources of this area were extensively used by the Pomo Indians who were among the finest basket-makers in North America. Archeologists have found Indian artifacts here that date back as much as 10,000 years. Examples of this archeological evidence are on display at the Anderson Ranch House and can been seen in the field during ranger-led hikes. The headquarters of the park was once a ranch headquarters, and is the only portion of the park accessible by automobile.

An easy hike will take you to an Indian village that is reconstructed each year by Pomo elders and others on an oak-studded knoll overlooking the marsh. The restored village also doubles as a picnic area, and the intermixing of picnic tables and tule huts is a

gentle reminder of the multiple tiers of history contained in this park. The park is open for day-use only. The ranch buildings are open for tours three days a week. In addition to visiting these sites, visitors come for bird watching, hiking, and picnicking. Summer field schools in archaeology for teenagers and others are conducted by the Cultural Heritage Council. (707) 994-4921. Anderson Marsh State Historic Park is located between Lower Lake and Clear Lake on Highway 53. (707) 994-0688 or 279-4293.

Napa Valley/Inland Sonoma County

Robert Louis Stevenson State Park

Robert Louis Stevenson State Park is primarily a hikers' park and features a five-mile trail that climbs to the top of 4,343-foot Mount St. Helena, a peak that dominates the northern end of the Napa Valley. The trail begins in dense woods and climbs to an exposed summit that offers panoramic views that include Mount Shasta, Lassen Peak, the distant Sierra Nevada, and the Napa Valley. The 3,694-acre park derives its name from Robert Louis Stevenson, author of *Treasure Island,* who spent his honeymoon on the slopes of this mountain in 1880. The summit trail visits the site of the Stevensons' cabin, though nothing of it remains today. This day-use only park is located seven miles north of Calistoga on Highway 29. (707) 942-4575.

Bothe-Napa Valley State Park

For thousands of years before it became a state park, Bothe-Napa and the Napa Valley as a whole provided food and shelter for a small group of native Americans known today as the Wappo. In the 1840s, Dr. Edward T. Bale, an Englishman, acquired an 18,000-acre land grant from the Mexican government including most of the land between Rutherford and Calistoga. Later developed as a large private estate, the 1,916-acre park today offers wonderful quiet and seclusion on the edge of the Napa Valley wine country, the park still provides ample opportunities for seclusion. Visitors can follow hiking trails alongside a perennial stream or climb to a vantage point 600 feet above the valley floor. Trails lead to nearby Bale Grist Mill State Historic Park or into a grove of one of California's easternmost stands of second-growth redwoods. The park has 50 developed campsites (nine of which are walk-in) and a swimming pool that provides an opportunity to cool off on summer days. Bothe-Napa State Park is located four miles north of St. Helena on Highway 29. (707) 942-4575.

Bale Grist Mill State Historic Park
When Napa Valley's early settlers harvested their fields of grain in the 1840s, Edward Turner Bale's water wheel-powered gristmill transformed it into flour for their household use. A physician and surgeon-in-chief of the Mexican Army, whose controversial personal life was peppered with intrigue, Bale received his valley property in a Mexican land grant and lived here until his death in 1849. The mill remained in use until the early 1900s. Today, the mill and its 36-foot water wheel, are protected as a state historic landmark and have been completely restored. The Bale Grist Mill is open every day from 10 to 5, and a helpful team of docents is on hand to explain the workings of the mill and answer questions. Call for a schedule of water wheel and mill demonstrations. The park is located three miles north of St. Helena on Highway 29 in Napa Valley. (707) 963-2236.

Annadel State Park
Annadel State Park encompasses some 4,900 acres of rolling hills, meadows, streams, and woods and is especially popular with hikers, cyclists, and equestrians. No paved road penetrates its interior, but there are 35 miles of trails and fire roads—many of them open to bicycles and horses. Centrally located trailheads include automobile parking facilities. Camping is not allowed. With elevations ranging from 300 to almost 1,900 feet, Annadel's varied terrain is traversed by numerous trails, offering easy to moderate hikes. Cobblestone quarries in this area once supplied paving material for San Francisco; the abandoned quarries can still be found along several trails. Annadel State Park is located east of Santa Rosa and south of Highway 12. Turn south

This vineyard is still operated by the heirs of the Jack London estate, Jack London State Historic Park.

on Mission Blvd, then immediately east on Montgomery Dr., and a mile later right onto Channel Dr. (707) 539-3911 or 938-1519.

Sugarloaf Ridge State Park
Sugarloaf Ridge State Park is primarily a day-use hiking park, offering 25 miles of trails that span an elevation range between 600 and 2,700 feet. Its 2,700 acres include a section of Sonoma Creek and the hills that border it; one-way hikes up to seven miles in length are possible within the park. The park also contains three summits that are accessible by trail; the highest of these, 2,729-foot Bald Mountain, provides a panorama that—on a clear day—includes both the Sierra Nevada and the Golden Gate. There is also a self-guiding nature trail along Sonoma Creek that starts near the campground, where there are 50 developed campsites. Horses are permitted in the park. Sugarloaf Ridge State Park is located north of Highway 12, seven miles east of Santa Rosa on Adobe Canyon Rd. (707) 833-5712 or 938-1519.

Jack London State Historic Park
This 800-acre park is a memorial to writer and adventurer Jack London, who made his home here from 1905 until his death in 1916. From his cottage residence in these tranquil hills, London poured out a tremendous volume of books, short stories, articles, and letters while also overseeing his ambitious agricultural enterprises. After London's death, his wife, Charmian, continued to live here until her death in 1955; it was her wish that the ranch be set aside in memory of Jack London and his works.

There is now a museum in "The House of Happy Walls," which Mrs. London had built in a redwood grove. A trail leads just over half a mile to the gravesite of Jack London and on to the impressive ruins of "Wolf House," London's dream house, which was destroyed by fire in 1913 just as it was completed. An upper parking lot, west of the museum parking, provides access to a picnic area, London's cottage, stables, stone barns, silos, and pig palace. From here a ¾-mile walk takes you to the dam, lake, and bathhouse London built. Longer hikes lead up through fir and oak woodlands enroute to rewarding views of the Valley of the Moon. Cycling and horseback riding are permitted on some trails, and guided equestrian tours are available. Camping is available seven miles away at Sugarloaf Ridge State Park. Jack London State Historic Park is located off Highway 12 in Glen Ellen, about 20 minutes north of Sonoma. (707) 938-5216.

Red-hot pokers in bloom, Salt Point State Park.

Sonoma State Historic Park

The last of California's 21 missions was completed in Sonoma in 1823, but hardly a decade had passed before the Mexican government instructed Mariano Guadalupe Vallejo, commandant of the presidio at San Francisco, to move his troops to Sonoma and secularize the mission settlement there. Vallejo directed Sonoma's successful development for a number of years until, in 1846, a group of American settlers—the "Bear Flaggers"—seized the unresisting town and imprisoned the General Vallejo. They proudly announced formation of the "Republic of California" and created their own flag— the Bear Flag—only to replace at few weeks later with the Stars and Stripes of the U.S.A. Vallejo was eventually released, and with his 175,000-acre holdings, political know-how, and military expertise, he continued to be a powerful personage in Northern California as a member of the State Senate and, later, as the mayor of Sonoma.

Visitors to Sonoma State Historic Park circulate through the streets surrounding the town's historic central plaza, viewing over a dozen buildings constructed between 1823 and 1855, including those from the Mission period. There is a fine interpretive museum, restaurants and shops, and the town's shady, open plaza—a good spot for picnics and relaxation. Nearby, the Vallejo family home, Lachryma Montis, is also open to the public. It is a lovely, old residence, fully restored and furnished with immaculate grounds and an invitingly cool picnic area. There are no camping facilities. Sonoma State Historic Park is located in downtown Sonoma on West Spain St. (707) 938-1578.

Petaluma Adobe State Historic Park

Petaluma Adobe was the center of General Mariano Guadalupe Vallejo's agricultural empire from 1834 to 1850. It sits atop a knoll in the midst of what was once Rancho Petaluma—66,000 acres of prime grazing and agricultural land, and one of several land grants received by the general. The sweeping, two-story structure was headquarters for a flourishing trade in cattle hides and tallow, as well as the raising of sheep, magnificent horses, and a wide range of other valuable crops. Half of the original adobe has been restored; the rooms and grounds display an excellent sampling of furnishings and ranch equipment from early California. There are shaded picnic tables with pleasant views of farmland and oak-studded hills. Camping is not permitted.

The Petaluma Adobe is located on the eastern fringe of Petaluma and can also be reached from Sonoma via Highway 116 and Adobe Rd. (707) 762-4871.

Sonoma Coast

Kruse Rhododendron State Reserve

Visitors to this park can get a firsthand view of plant succession following a forest fire. Kruse Rhododendron State Reserve preserves an old forest fire scar, now covered with thickets of coast rhododendron that burst forth with clusters of large pink blossoms from April through June. A short loop trail leads through one of the best clusters of rhododendrons and another five miles of picturesque trails wind among other sections of the 317-acre reserve. Visitors also find dense stands of second-growth redwoods that are increasingly shading out the sun-loving rhododendrons and completing the cycle of forest regeneration. There is no camping in the reserve, but adjacent Salt Point State Park has campgrounds. The reserve's entrance is near milepost 43 on Highway 1. (707) 847-3221 or 865-2391.

Salt Point State Park

Covering nearly 6,000 acres and a diverse variety of plant habitats, Salt Point State Park sprawls along 6 miles of the Sonoma Coast, reaching two miles inland to include elevations above 1,000 feet. Miles of hiking and horse-back trails follow the coast with its sandy beaches, wave-scoured rocks, tide pools, and an underwater marine reserve. Other trails range inland, visiting such North Coast oddities as a pygmy forest and a hilltop prairie. Wildlife abounds, including blacktail deer, raccoons, coyotes, and a variety of rodents. The park is also very popular among divers. For campers, there are two spacious campgrounds with 110 developed sites, as well as 20 walk-in sites, 10 hike/bike sites, and several environmental sites. The park is located 20 miles north of Jenner on Highway 1. (707) 847-3221 or 865-2391.

Fort Ross State Historic Park

Indians, Russians, Aleuts, and Americans all played a role in the history of Fort Ross, the southernmost outpost of a Russian presence in the Pacific Northwest, whose influence was ultimately felt as far south as the Channel Islands and as far inland as Napa County. It was in 1812, while the United States was preparing for war with England and Napoleon was advancing on Moscow, that 25 Russians and 80 Aleuts landed at a small bay on the Sonoma Coast and built a heavily fortified stockade to protect their claim against the Spaniards. They had come to develop a food supply for their Alaskan communities, and to hunt and trade for the sea otter pelts, which formed the financial backbone of their empire. They remained at Fort Ross until sea otter became scarce and in 1841 sold their entire holdings to John Sutter, who was later to become famous when gold was discovered at his saw mill in the Sierra Nevada foothills.

Today, only one of the original structures remains, but the stockade and three other buildings, including the first Russian Orthodox chapel south of Alaska, have been meticulously reconstructed in the 1,160-acre park. Exhibits and a self-guided audio tour help tell the story of this unique historic site. The visitor center is open from 10 to 4:30 daily; two miles south is a 25-site primitive campground. Located off Highway 1, the entrance to Fort Ross State Historic Park is 12 miles north of Jenner. (707) 847-3286 or 865-2391.

Sonoma Coast State Beach

A scenic stretch of coast that is sometimes compared to Big Sur, Sonoma Coast State Beach offers visitors a chance to explore a pristine seaside environment that combines high bluffs, beaches, and dunes. The park is also home to one of California's largest seal rookeries. With more than 10 miles of shoreline and 5,000-acres, this state beach is among the largest in the state.

At its northern end, just outside the official park boundary, the coast highway ascends steeply to a summit more than 600 feet above the water, offering stunning views of the park's dramatic shoreline. Further south is the mouth of the Russian River, a memorably scenic spot and the congregating place for dozens of seals and many kinds of seabirds. Near park headquarters is a two-mile-long beach, as well as hiking and horse trails meandering through 1,000 acres of dunes; 98 developed campsites are nestled along the dunes' edge. Tide pools, rocky bluffs and a 30-unit campground are found at Wright's Beach. Bodega Head, at the southern end of the park, is one of its most popular attractions. On a clear day the view sweeps all the way south to Point Reyes and Mount Tamalpais. In winter, Bodega Head is one of the finest whale-watching sites on the North Coast. Sonoma Coast State Beach is located between Jenner and Bodega Bay on Highway 1. (707) 875-3483.

Armstrong Redwoods State Reserve

In the 1870s, while lumberman Colonel James Armstrong was busy harvesting the dense redwood forests north of Guerneville, he decided to save the grove of ancient redwoods that now forms the heart of Armstrong Redwoods State Reserve—a primeval forest that Colonel Armstrong set aside to be preserved forever as an island of natural beauty. Today, a quiet road winds through part of the 500-acre grove, while short trails visit two trees each over 300 feet tall. Hikers who want to stroll through the cool, dense forest can enter, free of charge, from the parking lot at the ranger station. Horse rentals, for trips ranging from a half-day up to three days, are available for rides inside the reserve and adjacent Austin Creek

State Recreation Area. The reserve is located two miles north of Guerneville on Armstrong Woods Rd. (707) 869-2015 or 865-2392.

Austin Creek State Recreation Area

Austin Creek is a 4,200-acre recreation area with habitats that include steep, grassy hillsides, oak woodlands, pine-clad slopes, and riparian corridors lined with hardwoods. This diverse parkland, a distinct contrast from the neighboring redwood groves, nurtures a variety of wildlife, and counts many bird species among its residents, including wood ducks, great blue herons, and black-shouldered kites.

A hiker's and backpacker's dream, Austin Creek includes topography ranging from 150 to1,500 feet and 22 miles of scenic trails. For hikers and horseback riders there are several back-country campsites (permits required). Austin Creek's 24-site primitive campund provides a pleasant base camp for day hikes and is open to camper vehicles up to 20 feet (no trailers). The access road has only one lane (with turnouts) and climbs 700 feet in a single mile—effectively limiting the campground to tent campers. The road leaves from the picnic area of Armstrong Redwoods State Reserve, two miles north of Guerneville on Armstrong Woods Rd. (707) 869-2015 or 865-3483.

View of the old Russian chapel, Fort Ross State Historic Park.

(Above): Tent campers at Donner Memorial State Park. (Below): Backpackers make their way along a trail at Mount San Jacinto.

Environmental Camping

The California State Park System offers many excellent opportunities to learn how to backpack. Camping opportunities range from easy-to-reach, walk-in campsites to top-quality wilderness experiences at primitive trail camps.

Beginners and families with young children often enjoy walk-in camps. Usually located in one wing of a developed campground, walk-in camps are accessible via a short walk from a parking area. This type of campsite can be found in a number of state parks and can be a good place to learn what it is like to camp without immediate access to an automobile.

Primitive sites that can only be reached on foot are referred to as "environmental campsites." They are located in a number of state parks (see page —– for complete list). They are situated in scenic locations that feel remote—even on busy weekends. Many environmental sites are only one to three miles from the trailhead, putting them well within reach of the average hiker and allowing an easy return to civilization if the weather turns bad or you discover you've forgotten something.

A number of state parks offer more rugged wilderness hiking and camping experiences, as well as trails that can be combined to form lengthy multi-day treks; among them are Sinkyone Wilderness, Anza-Borrego Desert, Henry Coe, Humboldt Redwoods, Big Basin Redwoods, Cuyamaca Rancho, and Mount San Jacinto.

Here are a few common-sense rules that are followed by experienced and considerate campers.

- Leave your campsite clean. If you packed it in, you should pack it out. Don't leave food scraps that will attract animals, or deposit trash in a fire pit or pit toilet.
- Don't put food in your tent. Place food in a stuff bag and hang it from a tree limb, out of reach of raccoons, rodents, or bears.
- Travel light. This doesn't mean you have to spend a lot of money on fancy light-weight equipment, although that does help. The secret is simply to make the things that you carry serve as many purposes as possible.
- Always bring adequate clothing, including rain gear, regardless of the forecast. The best way to dress is in layers that can be combined to cover the entire range of possible conditions.
- Don't drink untreated water. Many backcountry streams, creeks, and lakes are contaminated with a single-celled protozoan known as *giardia lamblia,* which causes severe diarrhea, fever, and stomach cramps. Giardia—found in even the purest-looking mountain water—can be killed by boiling water for 10 minutes or treating it with certain chemicals or filters designed to eliminate it. Don't contribute to water pollution by washing cooking and eating utensils directly in streams, rivers, or lakes.

- Where pit toilets are not available, bury human waste at least 12 inches in the ground at least 50 yards from any lake or stream.
- Bring your own fuel or lightweight, portable stove; wood gathering is prohibited at most state parks. Properly extinguish all campfires.
- Leave pets at home.
- Carry a flashlight and make sure your batteries are fresh.
- Carry a first-aid kit.

Environmental campsites often need reservations, just like any others. For information, contact MISTIX at (800) 444-7275.

Hikers at Anza-Borrego Desert State Park.

CHAPTER TWO

Northern California Inland

The landscape of inland Northern California is large and diverse—a far-flung territory that might be called California's great outback. In the area that begins at metropolitan Sacramento and stretches north and east, there are whole counties whose populations could be gathered into towns that would still be thought of as "small."

The region's northernmost fringe is for people who like to explore, with enough scenery and wildland that thorough exploration could easily occupy a lifetime. Outlying parks like Plumas-Eureka, McArthur-Burney, and Ahjumawi Lava Springs are so remote that even the most cursory visit must take the better part of an entire day.

The heart of the region is the Sacramento River Valley, which on a clear spring day offers vistas of wildflower-strewn meadows and orchards, framed against the misty silhouettes of snow-capped mountains. The Sacramento River threads its way through the valley—a youthful, rushing stream in the north, a sluggish, meandering giant in the south. It is bordered by several state parks, including Bidwell River Park, Ide Adobe, Woodson Bridge, and Colusa-Sacramento River, where visitors will find easy access to the river itself, a number of historic buildings, and plenty of picnic areas and camping sites. Tributaries of the Sacramento River also offer a variety of recreational opportunities. The massive reservoirs at Folsom Lake and Lake

Oroville state recreation areas feature boating, water sports, hiking, and camping facilities, while Auburn State Recreation Area and South Yuba River Project provide access to miles of white water along the American and Yuba rivers.

In contrast to the subtle beauty of the Sacramento River Valley is the rugged grandeur of Lake Tahoe, which Mark Twain once described as "the fairest picture the whole earth affords." Three excellent state parks—Emerald Bay, D.L. Bliss, and Sugar Pine Point—and two state recreation areas are found along the shores of the world-famous lake. Within easy driving distance of the Lake Tahoe Basin are two other state parks in lovely alpine settings, Donner Memorial and Grover Hot Springs.

In the Sierra foothills east of Sacramento is the Mother Lode country, the fabled gold district that lured hundreds of thousands of settlers to California. Several of the most important gold mining areas are now preserved in state historic parks such as Marshall Gold Discovery, Empire Mine, and Malakoff Diggins. Visitors to these historic areas can trace the evolution of the gold rush from its beginnings in 1848 to the end of active mining in the mid-1950s.

In the modern city of Sacramento, several unusual and fascinating historic parks can be found within a few blocks of the California State Capitol. These parks span a full 150 years of Northern California history, ranging from the early settlement at Sutter's Fort to the

historic district of Old Sacramento and the California State Railroad Museum. Even the State Capitol itself has been restored to its turn-of-the-century elegance and includes historical exhibits and authentically furnished period rooms. Close beside Sutter's Fort is the State Indian Museum, which pays tribute to California Indian culture, both past and present.

(Opposite): Rubicon Bay, D.L. Bliss State Park.
(Above): Mexican period saddle, Sutter's Fort State Historic Park.

(Clockwise from bottom): Yellow lupine; Pioneer Monument, Donner Memorial State Park; a monitor for hydraulic mining at Malakoff Diggins State Park.

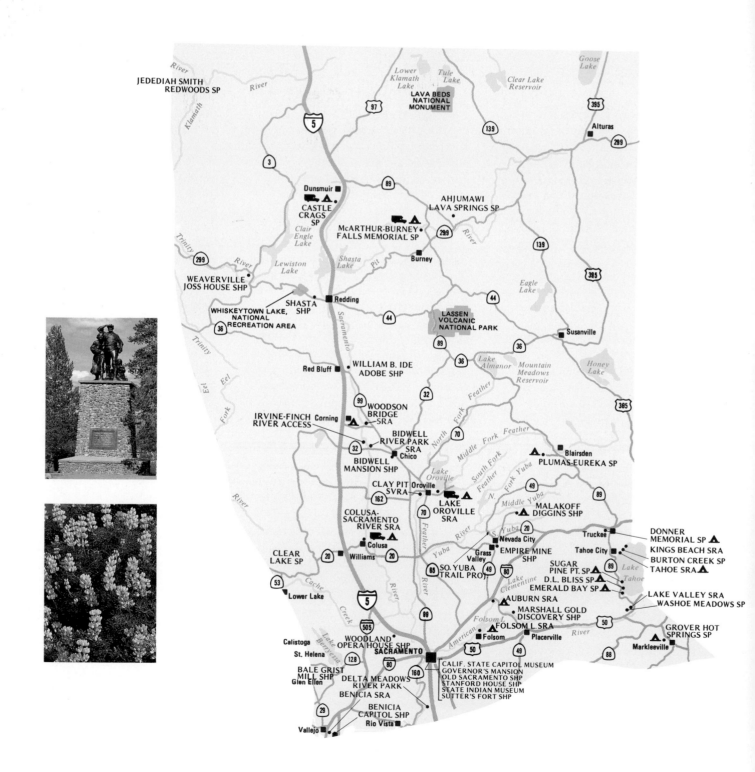

Redding Region

Castle Crags State Park

Castle Crags is a well-known landmark along Interstate 5 near Dunsmuir—a cliff face of dramatically sculpted granite looming thousands of feet above the valley floor and the nearby Sacramento River. In a largely volcanic landscape dominated by the great cone of Mount Shasta, the crags look like a misplaced fragment of the Sierra Nevada.

The 4,000-acre state park lies at the base of the Castle Crags, with vistas not only of the spires themselves, but also of Mount Shasta to the northeast. Traversed by 18 miles of trails, including a section of the Pacific Crest Trail, the park also features 64 developed campsites, horse trails, and picnicking, fishing, and swimming along the upper Sacramento River. Park rangers offer interpretive programs in summer. The crags themselves do not lie within the park, but are on private land. Castle Crags State Park is located six miles south of Dunsmuir. (916) 235-2684 or 225-2065.

Ahjumawi Lava Springs State Park

The word *Ahjumawi* means "the people who live near the waters." Ahjumawi Lava Springs State Park lies near the junction of three rivers, a creek, several sizeable lakes, and one of the largest systems of natural springs anywhere in the world. Located on the edge of the Modoc Plateau, a region of seasonal lakes and lava beds that covers much of northeastern California, the park contains the outlet of an underground river that drains Tule Lake, nearly 50 miles to the north. It is a landscape of unusual conjunctions, with spring-fed pools at the edge of porous lava flows, and flat marshes and lakes reflecting the sweeping backdrop of the southern Cascades.

With several miles of interconnected waterways, this 6,000-acre park is a paradise for canoeists and boaters and is a great spot for bird watching, especially during the autumn. Ahjumawi also contains several miles of hiking trails, but bring mosquito repellant and sturdy hiking boots if you plan to walk through the lava flows. Visitors can also view Indian fish traps constructed in prehistoric times and still maintained and operated by the Ahjumawi people.

There is no road access, nor are there any developed facilities other than nine environmental campsites. To get to the park, boats should be launched from a site known as the "Rat Farm." It can be found by turning north from Highway 299 on Main St. in the town of McArthur, driving past the fairgrounds, and turning right to continue 3½ miles on a dirt road. (916) 335-2777.

McArthur-Burney Falls Memorial State Park

President Theodore Roosevelt referred to Burney Falls as the eighth wonder of the world. Other visitors may be left speechless at the sight of this extraordinary, scenic centerpiece of McArthur-Burney Falls Memorial State Park. What makes Burney Falls so special is not its height (at 129 feet it is impressive though unremarkable by California standards) but rather the fact that almost 100 million gallons of water roar over the top each day all year long, while another large volume of water emerges out of the cliff itself in a broad line of springs that send feathery streamers cascading into the basin below. The spray from all of this water supports a lush growth of vegetation that looks almost tropical in contrast to the dark, volcanic rock behind it.

In addition to the falls, McArthur-Burney State Park also contains more than 800 acres of open pine forest, nearly two miles of Burney Creek, 128 developed campsites, and a small piece of shoreline on nine-mile-long Lake Britton, offering swimming, fishing, boat launching, and boat rentals. Due to the park's elevation (3,000 feet) and its northerly location, winters are cold. Most visitors prefer to come during the summer, but the spring and fall months offer a wonderful combination of good weather and quiet, uncrowded conditions. The park is located six miles north of Highway 299, on Highway 89 near Burney. (916) 335-2777 or 335-5483.

(Top): The misty peaks of Castle Crags State Park. (Above): McArthur-Burney Falls Memorial State Park.

Weaverville Joss House State Historic Park

Weaverville Joss House is the oldest continuously used Chinese temple in California. Above the door of this Taoist temple, Chinese characters read, "The Temple of the Forest Beneath the Clouds." Built in 1875 in the mining town of Weaverville to replace a temple that had burned down, it was placed under state protection in 1956 to preserve and restore the building and its unique contents. For some visitors, it is still a place of worship. The temple offers a fascinating glimpse of Chinese traditions and the role the Chinese played in settling the West.

A red frame building the size of an ordinary house, with portions of its exterior painted blue and white to resemble Chinese tile, the Joss House contains a richly furnished interior featuring ornate images of Taoist deities. Inside the doors are two large panels known as "spirit screens" that were intended to keep out evil spirits, which, according to traditional Chinese belief, could only travel in straight lines. Closed on major holidays, and on Tuesdays and Wednesdays from November through February, it is open by guided tour only. The schedule tends to fluctuate from year to year in response to public demand, so it is advisable to call for current schedule information. Weaverville Joss House State Historic Park is located on the south side of Highway 299 near downtown Weaverville. (916) 623-5284 or 225-2065.

Shasta State Historic Park

In 1849, as thousands of gold seekers were pouring into the Sierra Nevada foothills east of Sacramento, a second gold rush occurred in the geologically similar Klamath Range of northwestern California. Strategically located at the end of the road leading from San Francisco and the Sacramento Valley, Shasta, "Queen City" of the northern mines, became a prosperous shipping point and supply center. Goods were transferred from wagon to pack mule, stores sprang up, and prospectors came down out of the hills to spend their new-found wealth.

Today, this town—which was the county seat of Shasta County until 1888—still has several hundred residents, but its historic business district is a ghost town preserved as Shasta State Historic Park. A self-guided walking

(Top): Colusa-Sacramento River State Recreation Area. (Above): Woodson Bridge State Recreation Area.

tour helps visitors understand and enjoy the park. Many buildings are in ruins, but the courthouse has been restored and is open 10 to 5 daily; from November through February, it is closed on Tuesdays and Wednesdays. Exhibits include the fine Boggs collection of art by California artists. The park is easy to locate; Highway 299 passes down its main street, six miles west of downtown Redding. (916) 243-8194.

Sacramento Valley

William B. Ide Adobe State Historic Park

Just eight months after arriving in California from Illinois, William B. Ide became the first and only president of the state's short-lived Bear Flag Republic. On June 15, 1846, Ide delivered a rousing speech that was a catalyst in rallying the small band of American rebels after their capture of Sonoma. He was declared president on the spot and served in the office for 22 days until the "republic" became a protectorate of the United States. He later returned to his home near Red Bluff, where he served as a judge. The adobe house preserved today as William B. Ide Adobe State Historic Park is a memorial to this man. The park is open from 8 to 5 daily, and visitors are allowed inside the house. The home appears spartan by modern standards, but given the expectations of frontier California in 1850, it was snug and secure. The park overlooks the Sacramento River and is a popular picnicking spot. To get there, drive two miles northeast of Red Bluff on Adobe Rd. (916) 527-5927.

Woodson Bridge State Recreation Area

Woodson Bridge State Recreation Area includes some 428 acres of meadows and riparian woodland flanking both sides of the Sacramento River. Its primary attraction is for fishermen who enjoy the river's year-round fishing opportunities. The annual cycle includes shad, steelhead, striped bass, catfish, and three runs of king salmon between October and May. The park's west bank is undeveloped; the east bank contains a 46-site campground with spacious developed sites. The undeveloped portion of the park has a boat-in campsite for those who want to leave civilization a little farther behind. Adjacent to Woodson Bridge is Tehama County Park, which offers wading, boat launching, and picnicking. Nearby private facilities include a cafe and a general store. Both Woodson Bridge and the county park are located at the Sacramento River crossing on South Avenue, six miles east of Corning between Interstate 5 and Highway 99. (916) 839-2112.

Irvine-Finch River Access Site
Irvine-Finch River Access Site was created for a single purpose: to provide off-road parking for the inner tubers, rafters, and kayakers who use this popular section of the Sacramento River. In addition to its shaded parking lot, the five-acre park also has launching facilities for small boats. Raft rental is available for half-day trips, at least during the summer months. The access site is located at the southwest corner of the Highway 32 river bridge between Interstate 5 and Chico. (916) 342-5185.

Bidwell River Park Project
Although it covers 180 acres along nearly four miles of river front, Bidwell River Park Project cannot be found on most state maps. That makes it attractive to fishermen looking for some place new and different, although the area is well known in nearby Chico. Much of the park lies along a quiet slough of the Sacramento River, offering opportunities to canoe or kayak in calm water in an unusual setting. Other canoeists, kayakers, rafters, and inner tubers use the park as a put-in or take-out site for down-river trips. Tube rentals are available nearby. Picnicking is available, but bring your own water. There is no camping. To find the park, start at the river crossing for Highway 32 (between Chico and Interstate 5), then turn south on River Rd. a little more than a mile east of the bridge. (916) 342-5185.

Bidwell Mansion State Historic Park
Bidwell Mansion State Historic Park preserves the sumptuous home built during the 1860s by John Bidwell—early pioneer, social activist, congressman, leading agriculturalist, and a man who undoubtedly could have been

governor of California had the corrupt politics of his time not denied him the victory. Bidwell Mansion is a three-story Italian-style country villa with pink plaster exterior, 26 rooms, and 10,000 square feet of floor space. Notable guests included President Rutherford B. Hayes, John Muir, and many other leading scientists and public figures. Tastefully restored and furnished with a mixture of period pieces and original Bidwell possessions, the mansion today retains an atmosphere of comfortable, homey elegance that was a Bidwell trademark. Open to public tours from 10 to 5 daily (the last tour is at 4 p.m.), it is located at 525 The Esplanade in Chico, on the edge of the California State University campus. (916) 895-6144.

Colusa-Sacramento River State Recreation Area
Colusa-Sacramento River State Recreation Area has a long and rather checkered history. John Muir camped in the vicinity in 1872. Before that the area was used by the River Patwin Indian tribe, who lived nearby. In subsequent years, however, it became a city dump, and not until the land was given to the

state in 1955 was it transformed into the pleasant picnicking and camping site that visitors find today. The park's developed areas consist of lawns and shade trees on a bluff overlooking the river. Some undisturbed riparian habitat has been added nearby, bringing the total area to 67 acres. It has 18 developed campsites and launching facilities for small boats. The park is located within walking distance of downtown Colusa, nine miles east of Interstate 5 on Highway 20. (916) 458-4927 or 895-4303.

Woodland Opera House State Historic Park
The Woodland Opera House is the very last of California's once numerous, small town opera houses still being used for its original purpose. The original opera house was built in 1885, burned down in 1892, and was replaced by the present structure in 1896. Used only periodically between 1913 and 1988, it is now open once again on a regular basis for tours, theater, drama, dance, films, and special classes. The 644-seat opera house is located in downtown Woodland on Second St., between Main Street and Dead Cat Alley. (916) 666-9617.

Bidwell Mansion.

Gold Country/Sierra Foothills

Plumas-Eureka State Park

The cry "Eureka!"—which means "I have found it!"—has been associated with gold since the time of ancient Greece. It is no surprise, therefore, that 7,400-foot Eureka Peak in Plumas-Eurcka State Park sits atop what was once a large body of the precious metal. Mining activities began in the 1850s and continued until World War II. Today the miners are gone, leaving behind mountainsides honeycombed with 70 miles of shafts and tunnels and a number of historic mining buildings, including the Mohawk Stamp Mill, where millions of dollars worth of gold was processed.

The region now resounds with the happy cries of a new generation of Californians who have found their own form of gold in this hikers' paradise. With elevations ranging up to 8,000 feet, Plumas-Eureka State Park (6,700 acres) and its adjacent national forest lands include some beautiful high country, granite peaks, and dense coniferous forests. In the park there are more than 10 miles of trails, 67 developed campsites, a concessionaire-operated group camp that is accessible to wheelchairs, two fishable mountain lakes, a mining museum, and the partially restored remains of the stamp mill. It is also the site of what some have called the world's first ski lift, where miners wagcred on the outcome of downhill races on "Norwegian snow shoes." Skiing is still popular in the winter, and the park boasts a small downhill area, as well as opportunities for cross-country skiing and family snow-play. It is located five miles west of Blairsden on County Rd. A-14. (916) 836-2380.

Lake Oroville State Recreation Area

Lake Oroville is one of Northern California's great undiscovered secrets—a large lake that is almost never crowded. Although it has several miles of hiking trails, Lake Oroville is primarily a boaters' park, with 167 miles of shoreline at high water and more than 23 square miles of water surface. One arm of the lake reaches to within ¼ mile of 640-foot Feather Falls, one of the highest waterfalls in North America. For camp-

ers, there are two developed campgrounds with a total of 212 sites, as well as boat-in facilities. Launching ramps can be found in several places, and there is a developed marina at Bidwell Canyon, near the visitor center. One unique feature is a set of four "floating campsites" that are actually two-story houseboats moored in a secluded cove. The park is located seven miles east of Oroville on Highway 162. (916) 538-2200.

Clay Pit State Vehicular Recreation Area

The dam that forms Lake Oroville is the highest earth-fill dam in the United States. The clay used to build it was taken from the Feather River Valley, three miles west of Oroville. The resulting depression—a large shallow pit ringed with low hills—is good beginner terrain for off-road enthusiasts, and has been designated as Clay Pit State Vehicular Recreation Area. The 220-acre property also contains a rifle range. It is located on Larkin Rd, 1½ miles south of Highway 162, two miles west of Oroville. (916) 538-2200.

Malakoff Diggins State Historic Park

In the 1880s, Northern California was the scene of an environmental controversy so intense that it is surprising it didn't end in bloodshed. On one side were gold mine owners whose operations were worth millions of dollars—at a time when gold sold for just $16 an ounce. On the other side were the Sacramento Valley farmers and downstream communities such as Yuba City and Marysville. The issue was the operational technique known as hydraulic mining, which used huge streams of water to wash away entire hillsides in search of gold. It was very efficient, but it was so destructive that it sent millions of tons of debris down river, threatening to drown the valleys in mud. A court order effectively halted all hydraulic mining in California in 1884.

Today, in the Sierra Nevada foothills northeast of Nevada City, the largest and most famous of the hydraulic mines is preserved in 2,700-acre Malakoff Diggins State Historic Park. The park contains scattered pieces of mining equipment and the moonscape terrain of the huge mining pit. Visitors are free

to wander the trails through pine- and chaparral-covered woodland, stay at a primitive campground perched above the mine, or explore the remains of North Bloomfield and the exhibits that describe an otherwise forgotten way of wresting wealth from the land. To get there, take Highway 49 north from Nevada City. Turn right after 11 miles on Tyler Foote Crossing Rd. Follow the signs toward Graniteville; when the pavement ends, turn right into the park. (916) 265-2740.

South Yuba River

The South Yuba River Project is a major state park in the making. At present, it includes the longest single-span covered bridge in the world, four miles of the steep, rugged canyon of the South Yuba River, and a three-mile handicapped-accessible trail. When the park is completed, however, it will stretch from Malakoff Diggins State Historic Park to the confluence of the south and main forks of the Yuba, nearly 20 miles downstream. The park is now accessible by way of several different highways. The covered bridge lies eight miles north of Highway 20 on Pleasant Valley Rd. The handicapped-accessible trail, which follows the south bluff of the river, can be reached from Highway 49, one mile south of the river crossing, or seven miles north of Nevada City. Both the covered bridge area and the Highway 49 bridge are popular places for swimming and sunbathing. (916) 273-3884.

(Above): Nature has reclaimed its own at Malakoff Diggins State Historic Park. (Opposite): Empire Mine State Historic Park.

Empire Mine State Historic Park

As recently as 1956, the foothill town of Grass Valley was an active gold mining center. Many reminders of that era can be seen there even today. One of these is Empire Mine, which produced more than six million ounces of gold. The mine is preserved today as Empire Mine State Historic Park, offering visitors the opportunity to tour the surviving surface structures and to hike around nearly 800 acres of hillside perforated by 367 miles of tunnels, some of them nearly a mile deep. The main shaft is illuminated for its first 150 feet, and it is possible to peer beyond the lights into the murky depths.

The park also contains the "Empire Cottage," designed by Willis Polk for San Francisco financier and longtime Empire Mine president, William Bourn, Jr. This magnificent country manor is surrounded by beautifully restored gardens and grounds. The mine, the cottage grounds, and eight miles of trails are open daily, 10 to 5 (9 to 6 in the summer). Call the park for a schedule of guided tours of the house or the mine. Brochures with self-guiding tours of the grounds and mining areas are also available for purchase. After exploring the world of hard rock mining, visitors can return to Grass Valley or neighboring Nevada City to lunch on Cornish pasty—the traditional noontime meal of the Empire's Cornish miners—or stroll through the downtown which is filled with historic buildings, gift shops, and restaurants. The park is located at 10791 E. Empire Street. (916) 273-8522.

Auburn State Recreation Area

Encompassing some 42,000 acres, Auburn State Recreation Area features some 50 miles of river (much of it whitewater) on the North and Middle forks of the American River—including the rugged American River Canyon. The park also features about 50 miles of hiking and horseback trails. Although much of the park is accessible only by primitive road or trail, two of its most scenic areas are easy to reach. The first of these areas can be seen from the road that begins near the Highway 49 river crossing and climbs up the river canyon's north side; this drive offers wonderful views into the river canyon below. The other scenic area—just off this same road—can be seen from the Foresthill Bridge, which arches 730 feet above the racing waters of the North Fork of the American River. In addition to fine scenery, park visitors also enjoy picnicking, fishing, hiking, horseback riding, river rafting, and primitive camping. Lake Clementine is located 1½ miles off Foresthill Road and is a popular spot for boating, fishing and boat-in camping. Camping facilities are available on a first-come, first-serve basis. Parking in the Lake Clementine area is limited. Call ahead to determine availability. Development of park facilities has been minimal because the canyon may someday be flooded behind the controversial Auburn Dam. Bring your own drinking water. The main office for Auburn State Recreation Area is located on Highway 49, one mile south of the town of Auburn. (916) 885-4527.

Marshall Gold Discovery State Historic Park

In January 1848, James W. Marshall noticed some shining flecks in the tailrace of the water-powered sawmill he was building for John Sutter. "Boys," he told his co-workers, "I believe I have found a gold mine." As anyone familiar with California history knows, that was one of the great understatements of all time. Today, the discovery site is included in Marshall Gold Discovery State Historic Park in Coloma, along with a replica of the sawmill, a fine little museum, and a number of historic buildings. Picnic sites near stately groves of cottonwood and black locust trees are found along the South Fork of the American River. A monumental statue marks the gravesite of James Marshall, who died in poverty in August 1885. A brochure is available to guide you to the discovery site and other historic locations in the town. The park is located in Coloma, on Highway 49 between Placerville and Auburn. (916) 622-3470.

(Above): Ore wagons at Marshall Gold Discovery Historic Park. (Right): Fourth-graders pan for gold on the American River. (Opposite): Bodie, California.

Gold Rush

California's most famous gold rush dates to the morning of January 24, 1848, when James Marshall made his customary inspection of the sawmill he was building for John Sutter. During the previous night, Marshall had diverted water through the mill's tailrace to wash away loose dirt and gravel, and on that fateful day, he noticed some shining flecks of metal left behind by the running water. He picked them up and showed them to his crew, but while he was pretty sure that they were gold, the full significance of his discovery was truly impossible to imagine. He was still concerned about getting the mill finished.

Word of Marshall's discovery leaked out and immediately set off a "rush to the mines." By the spring of 1849, the largest gold rush in American history was under way. At the time of Marshall's discovery, the state's non-Indian population numbered about 14,000. By the end of 1849, it had risen to nearly 100,000, and it continued to swell to some 250,000 by 1852.

Gold was both plentiful and—by happy geologic accident—easy to extract, making the gold-bearing gravels of California's rivers into what has been described as "the finest opportunity that has ever been offered on any mining frontier." A contemporary newspaper put it slightly differently: "The whole country, from San Francisco to Los Angeles, and from the sea shore to the base of the Sierra Nevadas, resounds with the sordid cry of 'gold, GOLD, GOLD!' while the field is left half planted, the house half built, and everything neglected but the manufacture of shovels and pickaxes."

Today, a few mines and the remains of several boom towns have been preserved in a variety of state parks. Most of them, including the Marshall gold discovery site, the fabulous Empire Mine, the historic town of Columbia, the rich gold deposits at Plumas-Eureka, and the controversial hydraulic mining pits at Malakoff Diggins, are located in or near the Mother Lode region of the central Sierra Nevada foothills. While gold-seekers were pouring into the Sierra, deposits of the precious metal were also discovered in the Klamath Mountains of northwest California. Today, ruins of the historic town of Shasta and the Chinese temple at Weaverville Joss House State Historic Park recall the days of the Klamath gold rush. In combination, the Mother Lode and the Klamath gold fields produced the modern-day equivalent of more than $25 billion in gold before the turn of the century, with operations continuing at Empire Mine until as late as 1956.

Between the 1860s and the turn of the century, propectors found gold in a number of locations in California. One of the West's largest authentic ghost towns is Bodie in the eastern Sierra Nevada, now a state historic park that preserves the abandoned buildings of the rough-and-tumble mining town that sprang up in response to a gold strike in 1877. In Southern California, three historic gold mining areas lie within the state parks. Park headquarters at Red Rock Canyon State Park is on the site of what was once an important community in a region that produced several million dollars in gold, primarily in the 1890s—including one 14-ounce nugget. At Cuyamaca Rancho State Park, visitors can tour the remains of the Stonewall Mine, which produced $2 million worth of gold between 1870 and 1892. At Picacho State Recreation Area on the lower Colorado River, visitors can view Picacho Mill, the last visible remnant of Picacho, a gold mining community that boasted a population of 2,500 in 1904.

(Clockwise from bottom): Mouth of General Creek, Sugar Pine Point State Park; Catamarans at Folsom Lake; Snowshoe tracks at Donner Pass.

Folsom Lake State Recreation Area

The American River has been dammed near the town of Folsom since 1893, and hydroelectric power has been generated here since 1895 when the Folsom Powerhouse—once hailed as the "greatest operative electrical plant on the American continent"—first produced some 3,000 kilowatts of electricity. Today, both the original dam and the powerhouse have been replaced, but the historic powerhouse still stands and is open for tours.

Folsom Lake State Recreation Area's primary attractions are the lake and its beaches, where visitors can fish, swim, boat, picnic, and sunbathe. This park is also popular with hikers, runners, bicyclists, nature lovers, and equestrians, who use its 80 miles of trails, including a section of the Western States Pioneer Express Trail that connects Folsom Lake with Auburn State Recreation Area. For cyclists, a 32-mile-long bicycle path—one of the finest of its kind in the nation—runs downstream from the dam, connecting Folsom Lake with many Sacramento County parks before reaching Old Sacramento. The park also includes 500-acre Lake Natoma (just downstream from Folsom Lake)—a popular spot for crew races, sailing, kayaking, and other aquatic sports.

Three campgrounds contain a total of 180 developed sites, and there are a number of environmental camps that are accessible only by foot, boat, or bicycle. Folsom Lake State Recreation Area can be reached from several directions, but the simplest approach is to cross to the north side of the American River in the town of Folsom and drive north on Folsom-Auburn Road. (916) 988-0205.

Lake Tahoe Region

Donner Memorial State Park

To early pioneers heading overland to Northern California, crossing the Sierra Nevada before the onset of winter was a major concern. It was the failure of one such pioneer group, the Donner Party, to get over the mountains before the arrival of winter that led to one of the most tragic chapters in the history of America's westward expansion. After a harrowing trip across the Great Basin Desert, the ill-fated Donners were attempting to cross the Sierra Nevada when they were enveloped by a blizzard on November 26, 1846. Trapped just below the crest of the 7,200-foot pass now named in their honor, the group was unable to forge ahead. With food supplies rapidly dwindling, the group set up camp while several members of the party went for help. Word of their desperate plight reached the Sacramento Valley, but heavy snowfalls blocked the first of several rescue attempts launched from Sutter's Fort. By the time help finally arrived months later, 35 of the 82 members of the party had perished.

Today, Donner Memorial State Park commemorates their ordeal. The park's Emigrant Trail Museum (open daily, 10 to 4), recounts the Donner Party's story and features displays on the region's subsequent history and natural environment. The forested, 350-acre park is also a popular vacation destination, with 154 developed campsites, and opportunities for hiking, swimming, fishing, and picnicking, and cross-country skiing in winter. The park is south of Interstate 80, two miles west of Truckee. (916) 587-3841.

King's Beach State Recreation Area

Located on the north end of Lake Tahoe and boasting a scenic backdrop that is among the finest in the area, King's Beach State Recreation Area is a day-use-only park whose primary attraction is its broad, gently sloping beach. Visitors bask in the sun and water or play beach volleyball before a sweeping panorama of snow-clad mountains and deep blue water. During spring, the water near shore may be stained bright yellow-green by floating bands of pine pollen. On warm, sunny days, both local residents and tourists throng to this park, located 12 miles northeast of Tahoe City on Highway 28. (916) 546-7248.

Burton Creek State Park

The second largest of California's Tahoe-area parks, Burton Creek State Park covers 2,000 acres of presently undeveloped land on the outskirts of Tahoe City, somewhat removed from the lake shore proper. Six miles of unpaved roadway are available for hiking and cross-country skiing. (916) 525-7982.

Tahoe State Recreation Area

With 39 developed campsites and a small day-use area snuggled against the outskirts of Tahoe City, the tiny, 13-acre Tahoe State Recreation Area shares most of its waterfront with the cottages on the east side of Tahoe City. The park has a pleasant campground within walking distance of Tahoe City and is a fine place for a picnic lunch or a stroll on the pier with a magnificent view of the mountains and lake. The park is located just east of town on Highway 28. A half mile to the west at the Truckee River outlet to Lake Tahoe is the Gatekeeper's Museum, which features Indian artifacts and other North Tahoe historical exhibits. The museum is operated by the North Tahoe Historical Society. (916) 583-3074 or 525-7982.

Sugar Pine Point State Park

Sugar Pine Point is the largest of the Lake Tahoe-area parks, and the only one with year-round camping. With nearly two miles of lake frontage, dense forests with pine, fir, aspen, and juniper, and a cluster of historic buildings, Sugar Pine Point is a great place to spend a week or a weekend. The park offers many recreational diversions which can be enjoyed from its hiking trails, quiet beaches, fascinating lakeshore natural area, and cross-country skiing areas. The Hellman-Ehrman Mansion—also known as Pine Lodge—was an exclusive summer estate built in 1902 and purchased by the State of California in 1965; the mansion now serves as the park's visitor center. The campground is especially popular during July and August and stays open even in winter. There are 175 developed sites and 10 group camps that can accommodate up to 40 people each. The 2,000-acre park is located 10 miles south of Tahoe City on Highway 89. (916) 525-7982.

D. L. Bliss State Park

D. L. Bliss State Park, which borders Emerald Bay to the north, features one of the finest beaches in the Tahoe region. It also has several pleasant hiking trails, including the Lighthouse Trail and Balancing Rock Nature Trail. Because parking is limited, the beach fills quickly during peak summer

months; visitors are advised to either camp in the park (there are 168 developed campsites) or arrive before 10 a.m. Interpretive programs are offered during the summer. The park entrance lies a few miles north of Emerald Bay on Highway 89. (916) 525-7277.

Emerald Bay State Park

Emerald Bay State Park is one of the most scenic and most frequently photographed places in the world. The bay's rugged shoreline, brilliant blue-green waters, and high surrounding mountains have come to epitomize the grandeur that is Lake Tahoe's west shore. Vistas from the highway are spectacular, and there are parking areas that make it easy to enjoy the magnificent alpine scenery.

Hikers in the 590-acre park can head into nearby Desolation Wilderness or walk the rugged lakeshore between Emerald Bay and adjacent D. L. Bliss State Park along the spectacular Rubicon Trail. One of the park's unique attractions is Vikingsholm, an elegant structure of hand-hewn wood and sod roofs that has been described as the finest example of medieval Scandinavian architectural style in America. Vikingsholm is accessible only by boat or trail and is open for tours during the summer. Emerald Bay State Park has 100 developed campsites and is located 22 miles south of Tahoe City on Highway 89. (916) 525-7277.

Lake Valley State Recreation Area

At Lake Valley State Recreation Area the prime recreational amenity is a very fine public golf course. In a magnificent setting ringed by mountains, the Lake Tahoe Golf Course is a full-length, 18-hole championship-caliber course. Since the elevation is just over 6,000 feet, shots carry farther in the thin mountain air. In the winter, the recreation area has snowmobile and cross-country ski rentals. Lake Valley is located 3½ miles southwest of South Lake Tahoe on U.S. Highway 50. (916) 544-1583. Golf information: (916) 577-0788.

Washoe Meadows State Park

Washoe Meadows State Park occupies 620 acres of meadow and woodland in the valley at the base of the dramatic

escarpment leading to Echo Summit. Presently undeveloped, the park (unmarked) is adjacent to Lake Valley State Recreation Area, 2½ miles east of South Lake Tahoe on Lake Tahoe Blvd. (916) 544-1583 or 525-7232.

Grover Hot Springs State Park

Situated at an elevation of 5,800 feet on the east side of the Sierra Nevada, Grover Hot Springs State Park lies in a lovely alpine valley, surrounded by granite-topped mountains. Perhaps best known for its mineral hot springs, the park also has a variety of hiking trails and fishing along Hot Springs Creek and is a good spot for winter recreation, including cross-country skiing and showshoeing. For a modest fee, visitors can enjoy a small, concrete pool filled with 102°F to 104°F mineral waters or take a swim in the cold-water pool next to it. The springs are open in the winter, inviting visitors to relax in the hot water while looking out on snow-covered terrain. A 76-unit campground is open in summer, accommodating trailers up to 24 feet and RVs to 27 feet. From approximately October to April, camping facilities are limited to 17 sites, with no hot showers, and a maximum trailer length of 15 feet. The park is located 3 miles west of Markleeville on Hot Springs Rd. (916) 694-2248 or 525-7232.

Bicyclist at Emerald Bay State Park.

The California State Railroad Museum.

Sacramento Area

Old Sacramento State Historic Park

Old Sacramento contains much of Sacramento's original downtown. Unlike other historic commercial districts, Old Sacramento's period architecture is alive with shops and restuarants as well as historical exhibits—some of them in historic buildings that have been restored, others in new buildings carefully designed to blend and harmonize with the historical setting. The magnificent California State Railroad Museum is located next to the Big Four Building (an 1880s hardware store), the first theatre to be built in California, the building that was the western terminus of the Pony Express in 1860, and the first permanent home of the California Supreme Court. A self-guiding walking tour visits these and many other landmarks. Guided tours are conducted on weekends, when the buildings are open to the public. Old Sacramento is located between Interstate 5 and the Sacramento River, north of U.S. Highway 50. The Interstate 5 freeway exit for Old Sacramento is marked, and signs lead visitors on a circuitous route through downtown Sacramento's one-way streets to the park. (916) 445-4209.

California State Railroad Museum

The California State Railroad Museum, located on the edge of the Old Sacramento historic district, is a loving tribute to the role of the iron horse in binding California to the rest of the nation. Housing 21 pieces of rolling stock—including a number of old steam engines restored and polished to gleaming perfection—the museum is a railroad buff's delight and features locomotives dating back to 1862. Many of the showier pieces have been placed in dramatic exhibits, such as the full-scale diorama of an 1860s construction site high in the Sierra Nevada, or the bridge elevated 24 feet above the museum floor. One block from the museum are a reconstructed passenger station and a freight depot dating back to 1867, which contain more engines and cars.

During the summer months, a steam train provides excursions to Sacramento's Miller Park. There are plans to extend the service as far as Hood, 16 miles south of town, with possible return by riverboat, thus employing two of California's most important means of transportation during the 19th century. The museum is located at 125 "I" Street and is open daily, 10 to 5. (916) 324-4466.

Sutter's Fort State Historic Park

One of the most important figures in early California history was John Augustus Sutter, a Swiss immigrant who became a Mexican citizen in1840. In 1841, Sutter received a 48,000-acre land grant in the Sacramento Valley from the Mexican government. He named his ranch New Helvetia—"New Switzerland"—and managed the operation from the adobe fort he built on a knoll near what is now downtown Sacramento. It became the first non-Indian settlement in California's Central Valley.

Sutter was famous for his hospitality and for giving temporary refuge to travelers. In 1847, he sent rescuers to the aid of the Donner Party, trapped by the winter snows of the Sierra Nevada. During the Gold Rush, his fort was innundated by goldseekers and immigrants, some of whom swindled him out of his holdings or squatted on his land.

Sutter's Fort has been reconstructed to recall its appearance in 1846, two years before the discovery of gold. A walking tour, using acoustic wands, guides visitors through the fort's buildings and grounds. The park is open daily, from 10 to 5. Plan to arrive no later than 4:15 p.m., since the walking tour takes a minimum of 45 minutes. Sutter's Fort State Historic Park is located at 27th and L Streets in Sacramento. (916) 445-4209.

State Indian Museum

Long before the arrival of the first Europeans, California was home to an estimated 300,000 Indians belonging to more than 150 distinct tribal groups. The State Indian Museum portrays California's native-American cultures with displays that include Indian apparel, basketry, and beadwork, as well as exhibits about the ongoing cultural traditions of various California Indian groups. The museum also contains artifacts that belonged to Ishi, the last of the Yana Indian group in Northern California, who managed to remain hidden from western civilization from 1872 to 1911, until hunger and loneliness forced him to seek refuge among the whites. The State Indian Museum is located at 26th and K Streets in Sacramento, and is open daily 10 to 5. (916) 445-4209.

Governor's Mansion

The Governor's Mansion, or Executive Mansion, was originally built in 1877-1878 for Albert Gallatin, managing partner of a Sacramento hardware company. In 1903 the mansion became the official governor's residence and by 1967 had housed 13 governors and their families, briefly including Ronald Reagan, the last California governor to live in the mansion.

The mansion's interior design reflects a mixture of tastes, ranging from those of its original Victorian builder through those of the various governors and first ladies who resided here. It is open by guided tour only, from 10 to 5 daily. The tour schedule varies with the time of year, but generally the last tour starts at 4 p.m. The Governor's Mansion is located at 16th and H Streets in Sacramento. (916) 445-4209.

California State Capitol Museum

A tour of the California State Capitol Museum provides an interesting lesson in history and practical politics. Technically speaking, the museum tour only includes a visit to exhibit rooms located in the basement and first floor of the Capitol Building. In actual practice, however, the tour explores both the capitol's past and its present functions. If you are present on a weekday when the legislature is in session, there may be an opportunity to watch the legislators debate a bill or cast a vote. Guided tours are available on weekdays, 9 to 5; in fall and winter, tours are also offered on weekends, from 10 to 5. Visitors can also tour (with or without a guide) the 40-acre capitol grounds, which are landscaped with trees from many parts the world. The state capitol is located at 10th and L Streets in Sacramento. (916) 324-0333.

Stanford House State Historic Park

In 1857, wealthy Sacramento merchant Shelton C. Fogus built an impressive two-story brick residence on the corner of 8th and N streets. Leland Stanford, governor of California from 1862 to 1863 and one of the founders of the Central Pacific Railroad Corporation, purchased the mansion in 1861 and in 1872 remodeled and expanded it into the three-story house that stands today. The Stanford family made this their fulltime residence until 1874, when they moved to San Francisco. After moving, they used the house when business, politics, or social engagements brought them to Sacramento. Located only a few blocks from the State Capitol, the Stanford House is now surrounded by large office buildings. It is currently undergoing restoration, but guided tours are usually available on Tuesdays and Thursdays at 12:15 and on Saturdays at 12:15 and 1:30. (916) 324-7405.

Delta Area

Delta Meadows

Composed largely of a tule marsh and riparian woodland, Delta Meadows gives visitors a good idea of what the Sacramento River delta was like before reclamation of the area's wetlands began about 120 years ago. Its 140 acres of picturesque waterways and wooded banks offer ample opportunities for boating, fishing, picnicking, and bird watching. The park also contains the old Southern Pacific Railroad right-of-way, from Twin Cities Road to the Cross Delta Canal, where vehicles are allowed. There are no facilities or campgrounds on the right-of-way, but boaters find the adjacent waters a quiet and scenic place to anchor. Located behind the historic town of Locke is "Railway Slough," where boats may anchor for up to 15 consecutive days between Memorial Day and Labor Day for a maximum of 30 days per year. There are many fishing access points along Railroad Slough and a trail follows the water's edge. Vehicle access to the park is by way of a dirt road just north of the Cross Delta Canal, 100 yards south of Locke. The park is located one mile east of the town of Locke and can also be reached by boat via the slough. (916) 777-6671. **See also Brannan Island, page 72.**

Benicia Capitol State Historic Park

During its early years of statehood, California had a succession of "permanent" state capitols, first in San Jose, next in Vallejo, then Benicia, and finally, in 1854, Sacramento. Of the buildings that served as pre-Sacramento capitols, only the one in Benicia survives today. The interior of the Benicia Capitol has been restored with painstaking detail, including a board-for-board reconstruction of the building's original floor of ponderosa pine. The desks, three of which are originals from the Benicia period or earlier, are furnished with equal attention to detail, each equipped with a candlestick, a 19th-century newspaper, a quill pen, and a top hat. Benicia Capitol State Historic Park is open daily from 10 to 5 and is located at First and G streets in Benicia. (707) 745-3385.

Benicia State Recreation Area

Covering 720 acres of marsh, grassy hillsides, and rocky beaches along the narrowest portion of the Carquinez Strait, Benicia State Recreation Area's primary attraction is 2½ miles of road and bike path that are enjoyed by cyclists, runners, walkers, and roller skaters. Picnicking, bird watching, and fishing are also popular activities in this park. Vehicles may enter through a toll gate that accepts only quarters or dollar bills. Free parking is available just outside the gate. Benicia State Recreation Area is 1½ miles west of the outskirts of Benicia on Interstate 780. (707) 648-1911.

The Governor's Mansion in Sacramento.

(Above): The South Yuba River; (Right): Colusa-Sacramento River State Recreation Area.

California's Rivers

In October of 1877, John Muir floated down the Sacramento River from Chico to Sacramento aboard a skiff, which he christened "The Snagjumper." It was a restful trip, and he spent part of the time sitting in the stern reading as he drifted quietly with the current. According to Muir, a deckhand on a passing steamer commented, "Now that's what I call taking it easy."

In Muir's day, when America's rivers were extensively used for commercial transportation, California's navigable waterways were largely confined to the corridors between San Francisco Bay and the interior cities of the great Central Valley. A recreational trip such as Muir's must have been an unusual sight, and it is no surprise that people noticed him. Today, the rivers of California still serve critical roles in the state's economy, supplying hydroelectric power for cities and irrigation water for farms. But they are also recognized as major recreational resources, and their names—American, Feather, Yuba, Kern, Smith, Sacramento, San Joaquin, Klamath, Eel—form a litany that is rich in natural, historical, and recreational connotations.

Many of these rivers—along with countless tributary streams—flow through state parks and provide opportunities for everything from waterskiing to white-water rafting, from fishing to simply lying on a beach. California's many river recreation sites are almost too numerous to list: there are half a dozen big reservoirs, including those at Lake Perris, Folsom Lake, and Oroville state recreation areas, fabulous waterfalls at McArthur-Burney Falls Memorial State Park and elsewhere, untamed stretches of white water like those in Auburn State Recreation Area or Jedediah Smith Redwoods State Park, and smaller rivers like the South Fork of the Eel, which flows through Richardson Grove, Benbow Lake, Humboldt Redwoods, and several other parks, and features swimming holes in the summer and raging torrents in the winter.

For those who would like to repeat a portion of Muir's experience, there are six parks along the Sacramento River. To the south, the San Joaquin Valley boasts a number of fine riverside state parks and recreation areas that offer camping, fishing, or put-in and take-out places for boating expeditions of any length. And in the heart of the arid Colorado Desert, river enthusiasts can enjoy boating or floating along a scenic stretch of the lower Colorado River at Picacho State Recreation Area.

CHAPTER THREE

Central California Coast

Some of California's wildest and most beautiful coastline lies between the San Francisco Peninsula on the north and Point Concepcion to the south. The state parks of this central coast region are found along the beaches of San Mateo County, among the redwoods of the Santa Cruz Mountains, along the shore of Monterey Bay, amid the deep canyons and high bluffs of the Big Sur Coast, and among the great bays and rolling sand dunes of San Luis Obispo County.

South of San Francisco, Highway 1 winds along the coast through San Mateo County, skirting precipitous oceanside cliffs and hidden coves. South of Montara State Beach the terrain become less steep, the landscape fertile with farm lands and saltwater marshes. From Half Moon Bay to Año Nuevo, long stretches of beach are interrupted by rocky headlands that ensure a diversity of seaside recreational opportunities. The water here is rough and cold, and although swimming is not recommended, the tide pools, fishing, and wild breakers attract thousands of visitors to state beaches such as San Gregorio, Pomponio, Pescadero, and Bean Hollow. Wildlife enthusiasts seek out Año Nuevo State Reserve, a protected breeding site for the northern elephant seal.

Farther south, the coastal shelf slopes sharply up into the Santa Cruz Mountains where substantial winter rainfall supports vast groves of coast redwood. Big Basin Redwoods, California's oldest state park and the largest park in the

Santa Cruz range, was a focal point of the movement to save the redwoods at the turn of the century. Today, Big Basin and the other state parks in this range—Portola, Castle Rocks, Forest of Nisene Marks, and Henry Cowell—offer recreational pursuits such as camping, river fishing, hiking, and horseback riding, all within an hour's drive of the cities of the San Francisco Bay Area.

The coastline from Santa Cruz to Monterey, immortalized in the novels of John Steinbeck, was once a quiet fishing and farming area. Today, however, this picturesque region attracts tourists from all over the world. Swimming, surfing, fishing, and clamming are popular activities at the state beaches here, while Monterey, California's first capital, contains a large number of old adobes and other historic buildings that date from as early as 1792. A short drive inland, San Juan Bautista State Historic Park recalls several early periods of California history, while nearby Fremont Peak State Park offers camping, picnicking, and panoramic views.

The plants and animals of the Monterey-Big Sur region are well represented at Point Lobos State Reserve south of Carmel, where sea otters, harbor seals, and sea lions can often be seen from the trails. After the completion of State Highway 1 in 1937, the wild shoreline of the Big Sur coast gradually became a favorite destination for travelers. Today, visitors can sample the dramatic scenery of this famous coast at state parks such as Point Sur,

Andrew Molera, Pfeiffer Big Sur, and Julia Pfeiffer Burns.

The shoreline of San Luis Obispo County, from San Simeon State Beach to Montaña de Oro State Park, offers a variety of coastal environments, including high bluffs, secluded coves, rocky tide pools and headlands, sand dunes, and wide, driftwood-strewn beaches. Visitors to world-famous Hearst Castle can couple their visit with a stop in Morro Bay State Park for camping, golf, kayaking, bay fishing, or a trip to the outstanding Morro Bay Museum of Natural History. Farther south, the vast sand dunes of Pismo Beach and Pismo Dunes are popular spots for clamming, fishing, horseback riding, and off-road vehicles.

(Opposite): Fremont Peak State Park. (Above): Surfer, Santa Cruz.

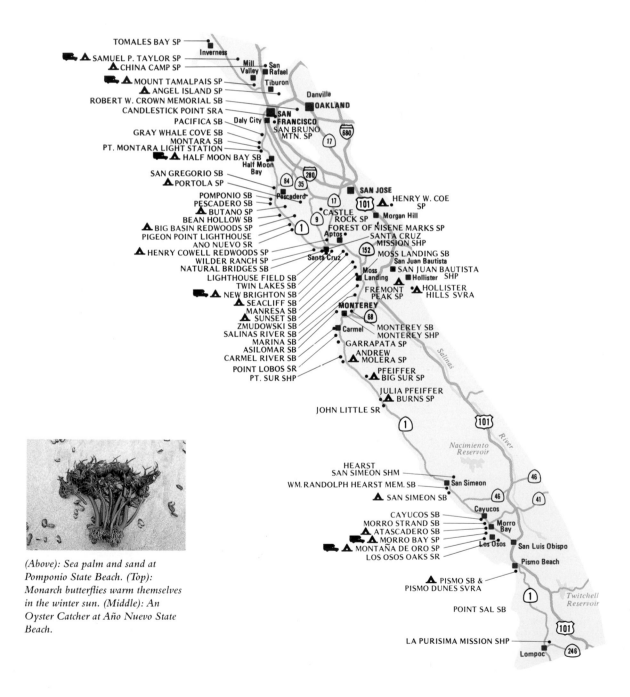

TOMALES BAY SP
SAMUEL P. TAYLOR SP
Inverness
CHINA CAMP SP
Mill Valley
San Rafael
MOUNT TAMALPAIS SP
Tiburon
ANGEL ISLAND SP
Danville
ROBERT W. CROWN MEMORIAL SB
OAKLAND
CANDLESTICK POINT SRA
SAN FRANCISCO
PACIFICA SB
Daly City
GRAY WHALE COVE SB
SAN BRUNO MTN. SP
MONTARA SB
PT. MONTARA LIGHT STATION
HALF MOON BAY SB
Half Moon Bay
680
SAN GREGORIO SB
PORTOLA SP
280
POMPONIO SB
94
35
SAN JOSE
PESCADERO SB
Pescadero
HENRY W. COE SP
BUTANO SP
17
BEAN HOLLOW SB
101
Morgan Hill
BIG BASIN REDWOODS SP
9
CASTLE ROCK SP
PIGEON POINT LIGHTHOUSE
FOREST OF NISENE MARKS SP
ANO NUEVO SR
1
Aptos
SANTA CRUZ MISSION SHP
HENRY COWELL REDWOODS SP
152
MOSS LANDING SB
WILDER RANCH SP
Santa Cruz
San Juan Bautista
NATURAL BRIDGES SB
Moss Landing
SAN JUAN BAUTISTA SHP
LIGHTHOUSE FIELD SB
Hollister
TWIN LAKES SB
FREMONT PEAK SP
HOLLISTER HILLS SVRA
NEW BRIGHTON SB
MONTEREY
SEACLIFF SB
68
MANRESA SB
MONTEREY SB
SUNSET SB
Carmel
MONTEREY SHP
ZMUDOWSKI SB
SALINAS RIVER SB
GARRAPATA SP
MARINA SB
ANDREW MOLERA SP
ASILOMAR SB
CARMEL RIVER SB
PFEIFFER BIG SUR SP
POINT LOBOS SR
PT. SUR SHP
JULIA PFEIFFER BURNS SP
JOHN LITTLE SR
1
101
Nacimiento Reservoir
Salinas River
HEARST SAN SIMEON SHM
46
WM. RANDOLPH HEARST MEM. SB
San Simeon
SAN SIMEON SB
46
41
CAYUCOS SB
Cayucos
MORRO STRAND SB
Morro Bay
ATASCADERO SB
MORRO BAY SP
Los Osos
San Luis Obispo
MONTAÑA DE ORO SP
LOS OSOS OAKS SR
Pismo Beach
PISMO SB & PISMO DUNES SVRA
1
Twitchell Reservoir
POINT SAL SB
101
LA PURISIMA MISSION SHP
Lompoc
246

(Above): Sea palm and sand at Pomponio State Beach. (Top): Monarch butterflies warm themselves in the winter sun. (Middle): An Oyster Catcher at Año Nuevo State Beach.

San Francisco Bay as seen from Mount Tamalpais State Park.

San Francisco Bay Area and Marin County

Tomales Bay State Park

Tomales Bay, a long, narrow gulf of blue water edged with tidal marshes, marks the line of the San Andreas Fault east of the Point Reyes Peninsula. The bay's sheltered coves are the primary attraction of Tomales Bay State Park, offering sunny, surf-free beaches that are popular with sunbathers, swimmers, picnickers, and nature lovers. The 1,850-acre park contains considerably more than picturesque beaches, however: it also boasts a beautiful grove of virgin Bishop pine, an abundance of wildlife, and several miles of hiking trails, including the ½-mile Indian Nature Trail, which shows how the Coast Miwok used the plants of the region in their daily lives. Nearby is Point Reyes National Seashore, which preserves more of the woodlands, beaches, and pastoral landscape for which the region is famous. Tomales Bay State Park is located eight miles from Highway 1 on the west side of the bay. Follow Sir Francis Drake Blvd. through Inverness, then turn north on Pierce Point Rd. after the boulevard climbs a hill leading away from the bay. (415) 669-1140.

Samuel P. Taylor State Park

In the 1870s and 1880s, the resort area known as Taylorsville was one of the first places in the nation to offer outdoor camping as a form of recreation. Visitors reached Taylorsville by narrow gauge railroad, and the area became one of Northern California's most popular weekend retreats. Today, the site of Taylorville lies within 2,700-acre Samuel P. Taylor State Park, which includes a 60-site campground and a mixture of open, grassy hillsides, rushing creeks, and cool canyon bottoms filled with redwoods and ferns. Popular activities include hiking, horseback riding, picnicking, and camping. Visitors can observe the fall salmon and steelhead runs in Papermill Creek, but because these fish have declined in recent years, fishing is not allowed. The park is located 15 miles west of San Rafael on Sir Francis Drake Blvd. (415) 488-9897.

Mount Tamalpais State Park

On a clear day, Mount Tamalpais State Park offers a dramatic 360-degree view that takes in downtown San Francisco, the Farallon Islands, and even the distant Sierra Nevada. In 1896 a recreational railroad was constructed—the "Crookedest Railroad in the World"—that required 281 curves in 8.1 miles to ascend the 2,571-foot summit. Today, the railroad is gone, but a paved road allows visitors to drive to the top. For the most part, however, this is a park for hikers and equestrians, with more than 50 miles of trail that ascend the mountain from various angles or snake across its flanks with views of the San Francisco Bay Area to the east and the blue Pacific to the west.

Mount Tamalpais State Park, the first part of which was acquired in 1928, is one of the oldest in the system and has a long history as a weekend getaway for residents of the Bay Area. Its 6,300 acres completely surround the stately old-growth redwoods of Muir Woods National Monument and contain many scenic and natural attractions. Park trails interconnect with those in the monument, as well as with 150 miles of other trails on land administered by the Marin Water District or the Golden Gate National Recreation Area. On weekends and holidays a bus line runs through a portion of the park, allowing visitors to schedule one-way hikes to or from the coast. The park is primarily designed for day use, but there are 16 developed walk-in campsites, 10 walk-in cabins, six environmental sites, and a group and backpack campground. Mount Tamalpais State Park lies along Highway 1 between Mill Valley and Stinson Beach. (415) 388-2070.

China Camp State Park

China Camp State Park preserves the site of the last Chinese fishing village on San Francisco Bay. It is also a fine place for swimming, boating, windsurfing, bird watching, and fishing; hikers and equestrians can explore meadows, woodlands, and coastal marshes that are typical of the ecosystem that once rimmed much of San Francisco and San Pablo Bays.

The centerpiece of the 1,640-acre park is the old fishing village itself, China Camp, where a small cluster of weather-beaten buildings and decaying foundations are all that remain of a Chinese shrimp-fishing village that was home to nearly 500 people during the 1880s. Several historic structures have been preserved, and an interpretive display describes life in the 20 to 30 similar fishing villages that once existed in the San Francisco Bay Area. Park facilities include picnic areas, a fishing pier and concession stand (open weekends only), and 31 primitive walk-in campsites. China Camp State Park is located four miles east of San Rafael and U.S. Highway 101 on North San Pedro Rd. (415) 456-0766.

Shoreline recreation, San Francisco Bay State Beaches.

Angel Island State Park

Angel Island State Park is located on the largest island in San Francisco Bay and offers visitors a chance to hike or bike through woodlands and meadows, sunbathe and picnic at protected coves, and enjoy fine views of Marin County, San Francisco, and the Golden Gate. The island boasts a fascinating history, having served at various times as a Civil War fort, a source for building stone, a major military embarkation center, a Nike missile base, and an immigration station in which Chinese immigrants were processed and often detained for weeks, months, or even years.

The 760-acre island can only be reached by ferry or by private boat and is circled by a mostly paved road that is popular with hikers and cyclists alike. Other trails crisscross the island and climb to the 781-foot summit of Mount Caroline Livermore. Attractions also include an assemblage of wooden Civil War buildings, the immigration station, and the remains of both World War I and II military bases. Camping facilities are walk-in environmental campsites. Dogs are prohibited on Angel Island. Check for ferry schedules, which vary with the time of year and day of week. From Tiburon: (415) 435-2131. From San Francisco or Vallejo: (415) 546-2896. Park information: (415) 435-1915.

Olompali State Historic Park

At one time, Olompali was the largest village of the Coast Miwok Indians. The recent archaeological discovery here of a 16th-century English sixpence indicates that the residents of this site met or traded with others who met Sir Francis Drake when Drake explored the region in 1579. Olompali's historic legacy will be more widely recognized and appreciated when this park can be opened to the public following the construction of a safe entrance to the park from the highway. Olompali State Historic Park is on U.S. Highway 101, three miles north of Novato. (415) 892-3383 or 456-1286.

Robert W. Crown Memorial State Beach

This East Bay shoreline location is complete with full day-use facilities and a visitor center. Operated by the East Bay Regional Park District, the beach is located on McKay St. in Alameda and can be reached via Webster and Central streets. (415) 531-9300.

Candlestick Point State Recreation Area

A pleasant bayside park with open lawns, Candlestick Point has two fishing piers, good windsurfing opportunities, a bike path, restrooms, picnic areas, and a fitness course for seniors. Located next to Candlestick Park, the recreation area is reached by taking the Candlestick exit off U. S. Highway 101 in San Francisco. (415) 557-2593 or 557-4069.

Gray Whale Cove State Beach

A steep trail leads down to this sheltered cove, which lies below cliffs that drop abruptly into the Pacific. There is a small picnic area on the bluff above, but no camping accommodations. Gray Whale Cove is operated by a concessionaire and is located north of Montara, on Highway 1. (415) 728-5336.

San Mateo County Coast

Montara State Beach

An inviting stretch of golden sand pounded by wild breakers, Montara State Beach is a day-use area bounded by low hills both to the north and south. Restaurants and grocery stores

are found close by. The beach parking lot is alongside Highway 1 just north of the town of Montara, 25 miles south of San Francisco. (415) 726-6238.

Point Montara Light Station

Built in 1875, Point Montara Light Station now serves as an American Youth Hostel site. The facility can accommodate about 30 people, and includes a laundry area, fully equipped kitchens, hot showers, a hot tub, and bicycle rentals. It's best to call ahead (evenings or early mornings) for reservations. The light station is just south of Montara, on Highway 1. (415) 728-7177.

San Bruno Mountain State and County Park

At the northern reaches of the Santa Cruz range, San Bruno Mountain and its surrounding 2,266 acres provide Bay Area urbanites with day-use facilities, hiking trails, and uncommon views of the city and the bay. It is home to a wide variety of birds and animals, as well as several endangered plant and butterfly species. San Bruno Mountain State Park, operated by the County of San Mateo, is located on Guadalupe Canyon Parkway in Brisbane, just south of San Francisco between U. S. Highway 101 and Interstate 280. (415) 363-4020.

Pacifica State Beach

This wide, crescent-shaped beach marks the northern gateway to the coastline stretching south of San Francisco. Operated by the city of Pacifica, the beach is for day use only and is located off Highway 1 in downtown Pacifica. (415) 875-7380.

Half Moon Bay State Beach

These two miles of sandy shore along crescent-shaped Half Moon Bay are a favorite weekend destination for camping, picnicking, beach play, surfing, surf fishing, and horseback riding on designated trails; swimming is not advised. Half Moon Bay State Beach consists of four locations—Venice Beach, Dunes Beach, Roosevelt Beach, and Francis Beach. Family camping is at Francis Beach, with over 50 sites, restrooms, and cold outdoor showers for rinsing off sand. There is a developed picnic area and ramp access to the beach.

Nearby private stables rent horses for trail rides above the beach. The group campsite near Venice Beach has a 50-person capacity. All four locations are just off Highway 1 in the town of Half Moon Bay. (415) 726-6238.

San Gregorio State Beach
San Gregorio Creek empties into the sea here, leaving a protected, drift-wood-strewn estuary at the back of a wide, sandy beach. From the spacious parking lot, footpaths head out onto grassy bluffs along the coast. The estuary, home to many birds and small animals, can be followed inland by passing below the Highway 1 bridge. San Gregorio State Beach is on Highway 1, just south of the Highway 84 junction. (415) 726-6238.

Pomponio State Beach
A wide parking area, picnic tables, bar-becues, a tiny lagoon, and roaring surf make Pomponio State Beach a great spot for a family or group gathering. Pomponio is 1½ miles south of the Highway 84 junction on Highway 1, just north of Pescadero. (415) 726-6238.

Pescadero State Beach
The mile-long shoreline at Pescadero State Beach includes sandy coves, rocky cliffs, tide pools, fishing spots, and picnic facilities. Just across the highway is Pescadero Marsh Natural Preserve, which is a popular spot for bird watch-ers and other naturalists. The beach is accessible from any of three parking areas, with the southernmost at Highway 1 and Pescadero Rd. and two others within a mile to the north. (415) 726-6238.

Bean Hollow State Beach
Wild and lovely Bean Hollow State Beach is a popular stop for those enjoy-ing the drive along scenic Highway 1. Visitors will find restrooms, paved parking, a few picnic tables, and two short curves of sand where they can stretch their legs, gaze at the turbulent surf, enjoy a quick snack, or make a day of it at the beach. Bean Hollow is lo-cated three miles south of Pescadero Rd. on Highway 1, with additional access a mile farther north at Pebble Beach. (415) 726-6238.

Elephant seal tour at Año Nuevo State Reserve.

Pigeon Point Lighthouse
American Youth Hostels operates an overnight facility at Pigeon Point that can house up to 50 people. There are showers, kitchens, and common areas, as well as a hot tub rental. The historic lighthouse, built in 1872, is open for tours on Sundays. Reservations are suggested for both accommodations and tours, with office hours limited to early morning and evening hours. Lo-cated between Half Moon Bay and Santa Cruz, the lighthouse is five miles south of Pescadero Rd. (415) 879-0633.

Gazos Creek Coastal Access
A sandy beach and a lagoon at the outlet of Gazos Creek are accessible here. Off-highway parking is available. Sun-bathing, strolling, fishing, and picnick-ing are popular activities. Dogs, motor vehicles, camping, and fires are not per-mitted. Gazos Creek is two miles south of Pigeon Point. (415) 726-6203.

Año Nuevo State Reserve
Año Nuevo, a 1,500-acre reserve, is best known as a protected breeding site for the northern elephant seal. The largest members of the seal and sea lion family in the northern hemisphere, elephant seals may reach 16 feet in length and weigh three tons. The dis-tinctively protruding trunk for which they are named is an inflatable nasal sac appearing only in the males. From December through April, the mam-mals breed both on the mainland and on Año Nuevo Island, just offshore.

During the breeding season, public access is restricted to daily guided tours, which must be reserved in advance and are held rain or shine. On the three-mile-long tours, California gray whales are often spotted offshore as they mi-grate between Alaska and Mexico. In all seasons Año Nuevo State Reserve is a wonderful place to savor fresh ocean breezes and an unspoiled environment. From May through November, the public is welcome to walk the reserve's many trails and enjoy the dunes, ocean, and wildlife. Bird watching is particu-larly rewarding in spring and fall. Park facilities, including a nature center and book and gift shop, are located in the farm buildings of the old Steele Ranch, one of the many dairies that dotted the coastal counties of California in the 19th and 20th centuries. The reserve is located just off Highway 1, 20 miles north of Santa Cruz. There are addi-tional access turnouts to the north along Highway 1 within three miles of the main entrance. (415) 879-0595.

Redwoods at Big Basin State Park.

Santa Cruz Mountains

Butano State Park

Only three miles from the coast, Butano State Park embraces coastal shrub lands to the west and rises gently eastward into the redwood forests of the Santa Cruz Mountains. Providing access to over 3,200 acres, the trails wind through redwood groves with views of the ocean and Ano Nuevo Island. Campsites are roomy and private; 21 are drive-in sites, suitable for RVs up to 27 feet long; 19 are tent camping sites, a short walk from parking areas. There is also a bike-and-hike camp. Back roads in and around the park are excellent for cycling. Butano State Park is five miles south of Pescadero on Cloverdale Rd.; it may also be reached by taking Gazos Creek Rd. off Highway 1, four miles north of Año Nuevo State Reserve. (408) 879-0173.

Portola State Park

Although closely situated to the Bay Area metropolis, Portola State Park seems far from the whirl of modern-day life. Secluded in a deep canyon, the park attracts campers, picnickers, and hikers alike, who revel in the relaxing solitude of its dense coast redwood, Douglas fir, and oak forests. A short, self-guided nature trail along Pescadero Creek is a helpful introduction to the area's natural history. There are over 14 miles of hiking trails covering 2,400 acres, including one path that meanders past a redwood tree that is over 300 feet tall—perhaps the tallest redwood in the Santa Cruz Mountains. Congenial staff members provide maps and information, as well as guided tours, evening programs, and children's activities during summer.

The family campground has over 50 tastefully situated campsites with nearby restrooms and hot showers. Campers and small trailers may be accommodated, but there are no RV services. There are several secluded picnic areas and a sizeable group site for both picnics and camping. A primitive, hike-in trail camp is provided for back-packers. Portola State Park is located six miles off Highway 35 (Skyline Dr.) along narrow and winding Alpine Rd. (415) 948-9098.

Castle Rock State Park

Along the crest of the Santa Cruz Mountains, Castle Rock State Park embraces 3,600 acres of coast redwood, Douglas-fir, and madrone forest, most of which has been left in its wild, natural state. Steep canyons are sprinkled with unusual rock formations that are popular with rock climbers. The forest here is lush and mossy, crisscrossed by 32 miles of hiking and horseback riding trails. They are part of an even more extensive trail system that links the Santa Clara and San Lorenzo valleys with Castle Rock, Big Basin Redwoods State Park, and the Pacific Coast.

Primitive campsites for backpackers are the only overnight facilities. Equestrians are urged to call ahead for current trail information, and smokers are advised that, due to high fire hazard, smoking is prohibited on the trails within Castle Rock State Park. Dogs are not allowed on the trails or in the campground. The park is located on Highway 35, just 2½ miles southeast of the junction with Highway 9. (408) 867-2952.

Big Basin Redwoods State Park

The oldest state park in California, Big Basin Redwoods was the focus of a major campaign to save an outstanding example of virgin coast redwood forest from logging. Citizen groups, private donations, and state funding have allowed for steady expansion of the park so that today it covers over 16,000 acres of redwood and mixed evergreen forest, chaparral, and coastal marsh lands. The 80-mile trail system, serving hikers and equestrians, connects Big Basin Redwoods State Park to Castle Rock State Park and the eastern reaches of the Santa Cruz range. Detailed topographical trail maps are available. Originating at Saratoga Gap (Highway 9 and Highway 35), the Skyline to the Sea Trail threads its way down through Big Basin Redwoods along Waddell Creek to the beach and adjacent Theodore J. Hoover Natural Preserve, a freshwater marsh.

At the coast, Waddell Beach is now a popular windsurfing site. The peak season here is from May to October. Heavy rains often fall in the off-season and Big Basin's trails and campgrounds are rarely crowded during those months. Camping facilities include 147 family campsites, five group sites, 36 tent cabins, and six trail camps. There is also a picnic area and a fine little interpretive center. The store, gift shop, and snack bar operate only during the summer. Located on Highway 236, the entrance to Big Basin Redwoods State Park is 9 miles northwest of the town of Boulder Creek. (408) 338-6132.

Henry Cowell Redwoods State Park

Situated in the lower elevations of the Santa Cruz Mountains, Henry Cowell Redwoods State Park is known for its good weather, excellent day-use area, and camping among ponderosa pines. The picnic grounds, suitable for families or large groups, are set above the San Lorenzo River. Fishing is also popular along the San Lorenzo, but is allowed only during winter months when the salmon and steelhead are running.

A nature center, gift shop, and coffee shop are nearby. From the nature center, a very gentle self-guiding nature trail leads through the redwood grove. The 4,000-acre park has 15 miles of hiking and riding trails. The campground—with showers and flush toilets—has a bike camp and 112 family sites, some spacious enough for RVs up to 36 feet long. Although the campground is linked to the day-use area by trails, vehicles must enter the campground east of Felton, via Graham Hill Rd. The main entrance and day-use area of Henry Cowell Redwoods State Park are located just south of Felton on Highway 9. Day use: (408) 335-4598. Campground: (408) 438-2396. District office: (408) 335-9145.

Home of Melvin and Letitia Wilder, Wilder Ranch State Historic Park.

The Forest of Nisene Marks State Park

Until the 1920s, logging operators worked full time at harvesting the great redwood forests of the Santa Cruz Mountains. Now, near the town of Aptos, nearly 10,000 acres of previously logged forest lands have been preserved in Nisene Marks State Park. This park remains largely undeveloped, as stipulated by members of the Marks family, who donated the land to the State of California in 1963. Thirty miles of trails traverse canyons and ridges, with scenic views in all directions at various points; they also pass a number of historic sites from the logging days. There are several picnic grounds in the lower reaches of the forest; the only campground is a trail camp six miles out along Westridge Trail. Space must be reserved in advance, and no drinking water is available. The entrance to The Forest of Nisene Marks State Park is on Aptos Creek Rd. in Aptos. (408) 335-4598 or 335-9106.

Monterey Bay Area

Wilder Ranch State Historic Park

Originally the main rancho supplying Santa Cruz Mission, 4,000-acre Wilder Ranch later became a successful and innovative dairy ranch. The charming ranch headquarters and surrounding grounds are a photographer's paradise, with fascinating barns, Victorian homes, lovely gardens, and a historic adobe. Guided tours of the blacksmith shop and the completely refurbished Wilder home are available. Call (408) 423-0746 (between 10 and 4) for reservations. Set amidst fertile, coastal lands just north of Santa Cruz, Wilder Ranch State Historic Park is immediately west of Highway 1, just a mile or so past the Western Dr. stoplight. (408) 688-3241.

Natural Bridges State Beach

A wide, crescent-shaped beach on the north side of Santa Cruz, Natural Bridges State Beach is named for water-worn rock formations just off the bluffs near the parking area. The shore is backed by a eucalyptus grove, where migrating monarch butterflies arrive by the thousands each fall. A nature trail winds through the trees; guided tours are available in the fall. Monarch Day is traditionally celebrated each year on the second weekend of October. Take Swift Ave. west from Highway 1, or follow West Cliff Dr. north along the in-town bluffs until it ends at Natural Bridges. (408) 423-4609 or 688-3241.

Santa Cruz Mission State Historic Park

Built in 1791, the Neary-Rodriguez Adobe was part of the complex of buildings erected around the original Santa Cruz Mission. This lovely, single-story adobe has been restored to its original appearance. In downtown Santa Cruz, take Mission St. to Mission Plaza; the adobe is located one block off the plaza on School St. (408) 688-3241.

Lighthouse Field State Beach

This open, grassy field across from Lighthouse Point, with a full view of Monterey Bay, is a terrific spot for a seaside picnic. Across the street from the park is renowned Steamer Lane, where large breakers attract surfers and observers alike. A surfing display is housed in the lighthouse. Offshore, a colony of noisy sea lions can usually be observed. Lighthouse Field State Beach is on West Cliff Dr. in downtown Santa Cruz and is operated by the City of Santa Cruz. (408) 429-3777.

Twin Lakes State Beach

This mile of sandy shoreline is a favorite swimming and picnicking spot. A snack bar and lifeguard station are located nearby. The park's two adjacent lagoons are excellent locations for bird watching. The small craft harbor in downtown Santa Cruz is roughly in the middle of Twin Lakes State Beach, which extends for some distance along East Cliff Drive. (408) 688-3241.

New Brighton State Beach

This popular park boasts an inviting, sandy beach with fire pits for day or evening picnics. Visitors return year after year to this seaside retreat for fishing, beach activities, and camping on a wooded bluff overlooking northern Monterey Bay. There are more than 100 developed sites for tent camping or RVs up to 31 feet long, as well as a camp for bicyclists—all with hot showers. In summer there are regular campfire programs on the natural history of the coastal region. Campground reservations are recommended year-round. New Brighton State Beach is in the town of Capitola just south of Santa Cruz and can be reached by taking the New Brighton/Park Ave. exit off Highway 1. (408) 475-4850 or 688-3241.

Seacliff State Beach

Warm summer weather invariably sends large numbers of visitors to Seacliff State Beach, where they can enjoy a long stretch of sand backed by bluffs, good swimming areas, and covered picnic facilities. Pier fishing is extremely popular here, with an old concrete freighter, the *Palo Alto,* forming a unique extension to the Seacliff pier. An interpretive center is located near the entrance to the beach-level parking area; adjacent is a 26-site RV park with hook-ups and showers. Advance reservations are strongly recommended. Take the Seacliff turnoff from Highway 1 in the town of Aptos. (408) 688-3222 or 688-3241.

Manresa State Beach

This beautiful expanse of sea and sand offers great surf fishing, clamming, and beach play. There are no facilities, but a lifeguard is on duty during the summer. From Highway 1 just south of Aptos, San Andreas Rd. heads west and continues for several miles to Manresa, the first beach access upon reaching the coast. (408) 724-1266 or 688-3241.

Sunset State Beach

Quiet, pine-studded campgrounds, mountainous sand dunes, and ocean-side picnicking make Sunset State Beach a favored destination for thousands of year-round visitors. Located between the cities of Monterey and Santa Cruz and bordered by vast agricultural fields, Sunset captures the rural, relaxed flavor of central Monterey Bay. The campground is protected from stiff ocean breezes by tall dunes and includes 90 family sites, a group area, a hike-and-bike camp, and hot showers. Trailers and campers up to 31 feet long can be accommodated. Just over the dunes lie miles of beach for surf fishing, beachcombing, and superb bay views. A path leads across the dunes to the beach, where day-use parking and picnic facilities are located. Take San Andreas Rd. off Highway 1, and go four miles past Manresa State Beach to a turnoff marked for Sunset State Beach. (408) 724-1266 or 688-3241.

Moss Landing State Beach

The calm waters of Elkhorn Slough open into a small, colorful harbor at Moss Landing that is protected by the dunes of Moss Landing State Beach. One of the most popular surfing beaches on Monterey Bay, Moss Landing is also a good locale for surf fishing, windsurfing, or horseback riding. With fine views and protection from the afternoon winds, the harbor's shoreline is an ideal picnic spot. Nearby are excellent opportunities for bird watching. The Moss Landing Harbormaster operates a boat-launching ramp just outside the state beach. The well-marked park entrance is just off Highway 1 on the north side of Moss Landing Harbor. (408) 384-7695 or 649-2836.

Zmudowski State Beach

An out-of-the-way fishing spot, Zmudowski State Beach is surrounded by farm land and backed by a small estuary. Horseback riding is allowed on the beach, but not on the dunes. A natural preserve on the north edge of the beach protects a nesting area for snowy plovers near the mouth of the Pajaro River. Facilities are limited to chemical toilets in the parking area and a boardwalk over the dunes to the shore. The beach is reached via Highway 1 and Sturve Rd., a mile north of Moss Landing. (408) 384-7695 or 649-2836.

Salinas River State Beach

A popular fishing spot, Salinas River State Beach protects one of Monterey Bay's most interesting sand dune areas. Horseback riding is allowed on the

(Top): Monterey State Beach. (Above): New Brighton State Beach. (Opposite): Hang-glider launching ramp, Marina State Beach.

beach. Two parking lots provide access to Salinas River State Beach. One parking lot is at the end of Potrero Rd., just off Highway 1 on the south side of Moss Landing. The other lot is off the Madera Road exit from Highway 1, south of Potrero Road. (408) 384-7695 or 649-2836.

Marina State Beach

Hang-gliding lessons and a hang glider launch pad make a colorful addition to the recreational activities at Marina State Beach. Other activities include surfing, surf fishing, sand-castle building, sunbathing, and simply watching the incessant tumble of the waves. The ocean can be rough at this beach; use caution when near the water. Reached by taking the Marina exit off Highway 1, Marina State Beach is just 10 miles north of Monterey. (408) 384-7695 or 649-2836.

Monterey State Beach

In Monterey, with its exciting waterfront and historic downtown, visitors and residents alike appreciate the quiet sands of Monterey State Beach, which stretches north from Fisherman's Wharf. This flat beach, along a relatively calm stretch of water, is a fine location for a long walk. Access at Del Monte Ave. and Camino Aguajito is poorly marked, and there is no designated parking. A few miles north, where the towns of Monterey and Seaside meet, Sand Dunes Rd. ends at Monterey State Beach, where limited roadside parking allows access to the beach and nearby picnic facilities. (408) 384-7695.

Monterey State Historic Park

Montery was the capital of California from 1775 to 1850 under Spanish, Mexican, and early U.S. rule. Today, many adobes and other historic buildings still stand throughout the dowtown area. The Old Custom House, the Cooper-Molera Complex, Pacific House, and the other historic buildings are open to the public. History and architecture enthusiasts should be sure to save a day for an unhurried walk along Monterey's "Path of History." A self-guiding brochure is available.

Guided tours take visitors through the Robert Louis Stevenson House, the Larkin House, the Cooper-Molera Complex, Casa Soberanes, and the Custom House, which is California State Historic Landmark No. 1 and the oldest government building on the Pacific Coast. The best starting point for your tour of historic Monterey is the visitor center in the old adobe Pacific House on Custom House Plaza. From Highway 1, take the Central Monterey exit and follow signs to Fisherman's Wharf; Custom House Plaza is directly adjacent to the wharf entrance. (408) 649-7118.

San Juan Bautista Area

San Juan Bautista State Historic Park

This historic park overlooks the fertile San Benito Valley and is situated in modern-day San Juan Bautista, a delightful little community with inviting shops and restaurants. Preserved and restored here are the original town plaza, the old Plaza Hotel, the Mexican Period home of Jose Castro, and a couple of early American Period buildings: Plaza Hall and the old livery stable. The pueblo was a military and commercial center during the Mexican administration of the California territory under Jose Castro. After the United States laid claim to the territory, a two-story adobe home built by the Castro family was purchased by the Breens, who survived the famous Donner Party tragedy in 1846 and whose son later struck it rich in the California gold fields. The old Castro-Breen Adobe now houses furnishings from the 1870s and is a fascinating introduction to the daily life of American settlers. Next door, the Plaza Hotel was a famous stop for travelers arriving by stagecoach. Many well-preserved carriages and coaches are on display in the old stable.

Mission San Juan Bautista on the north side of the plaza was founded in 1797 and is now a parish church. Mass is still held, but there is also a small history museum. Tours are available with advance arrangements. The nearest state camping facility is 11 miles away at Fremont Peak State Park. San Juan Bautista is located on State Route 156, seven miles west of Hollister. The turnoff to San Juan Bautista from U.S. 101 (between Gilroy and Salinas) is well marked. (408) 623-4881.

Fremont Peak State Park

A few miles south of San Juan Bautista, Brevet Captain John C. Fremont and his company of adventurers raised the American flag atop the tallest peak in the vicinity, disobeying the Mexican government's insistence that they clear out of California. Today, the mountaintop (elevation 3,169 feet) is a state park with primitive camping in a 25-site family campground, several group camps, an equestrian camp, and picnic facilities. The pine and oak woodlands atop the peak are alive with birds and small animals. Fremont Peak State Park also boasts an astronomical observatory that is open for public programs on selected evenings. A trail from the upper parking lot leads to the top of the peak, from where there are tremendous views of the San Benito Valley, Salinas Valley, Monterey Bay, and the Santa Lucia Mountains east of Big Sur. To get there, take San Juan Canyon Rd. and follow the signs for 11 miles south from San Juan Bautista and Highway 156. Trailers not recommended. (408) 623-4255 or 623-4526.

(Top): A ranger conducts a nature walk at Asilomar State Beach. (Above): A cobalt sponge at Point Lobos State Reserve.

Hollister Hills State Vehicular Recreation Area

Motorcyclists and 4x4 enthusiasts from the Bay Area and San Joaquin Valley enjoy this extensive, centrally located off-road park. Hollister Hills State Vehicular Recreation Area includes 3,200 acres and 140 miles of trail in two locations. For safety reasons there are separate areas for motorcycles, ATCs, and 4-WD vehicles. Self-guiding natural history walks through Azalea Canyon and along the San Andreas Fault offer added interest to visitors. Sites in any of four campgrounds are available on a first-come, first-serve basis. Group camps and locations for special events must be reserved well in advance. It is a good idea to call ahead and make sure a special event is not scheduled in a specific riding area you may wish to use. Hollister Hills State Vehicular Recreational Area is about six miles south of Hollister on Cienega Rd. (408) 637-3874.

Carmel and Big Sur Coast

Asilomar State Beach and Conference Grounds

Since 1913, Asilomar has been offering visitors a unique opportunity to gather and confer in a quiet and extremely beautiful natural setting. Julia Morgan, the extraordinarily gifted, well-known architect of Hearst Castle, designed Asilomar's first buildings for use as a YWCA summer retreat. Working in the Arts and Crafts style, she employed stone and other native building materials to create an informal yet elegant conference center.

In 1956, unable to afford the upkeep and unwilling to see the area developed commercially, the YWCA sold Asilomar to the State of California, Department of Parks and Recreation. Today the conference grounds are operated by the Pacific Grove-Asilomar Operating Corporation. Facilities include meeting rooms, recreational facilities, dining facilities, and guest accommodations for groups, large or small. Individuals may make room reservations up to 30 days prior to their proposed visit.

State park staff members protect the unique natural and cultural setting of Asilomar and conduct interpretive programs. Access to Asilomar is by way of Highway 68, which intersects Highway 1 just south of Monterey, or by way of Ocean View Blvd. west and south along the coast from Cannery Row in Monterey. A boardwalk across the dunes gives access to the beach and tide pool area from the conference grounds. Conference grounds: (408) 372-8016. Beach: (408) 372-4076.

Carmel River State Beach

Just before it empties into the sea, Carmel River opens out into a small lagoon and bird sanctuary—a wonderful setting for leisurely walks and bird watching. At the shore, the bracing salt air and coarse sand make this mile of coastline ideal for an invigorating walk or just gazing out to sea and soaking it all in. Ocean swimming and wading are extremely hazardous. The easiest access to Carmel River State Beach is found two miles south of Carmel; parking is alongside Highway 1. There is also a parking lot at the northern entrance off Scenic Dr., which follows the contours along the coast from central Carmel. (408) 624-4909.

Point Lobos State Reserve

Prior to the turn of the century, Point Lobos was the site of a shore whaling station, an abalone cannery, and the homes of immigrant Chinese, Japanese, and Portuguese fishermen. Today, only a single cabin remains at the once-busy little port of Whalers Cove. To the delight of park visitors, the bountiful wildlife that previously inhabited Point Lobos has returned, and the dramatic coastline is both wild and incredibly beautiful. The reserve's 550 acres are laced with trails that pass through forest and meadow, along the rocky coastline, and to the shore itself. Visitors can watch sea lions, harbor seals, gray whales, sea otters, numerous land animals, and countless birds in this unique and memorable natural habitat. A 700-acre, offshore underwater reserve allows divers to explore a completely protected, unusually diverse and beautiful underwater environment.

Each season at Point Lobos has its particular attraction, but perhaps spring—with its wildflowers, seal pups, and nesting birds—is the most captivating time for a visit. January is the choice month for whale watching, although gray whales may be spotted any time

Andrew Molera State Park

The Big Sur River meanders through the meadows and woodlands of Andrew Molera State Park on its way to the sea at Molera Point. The park's 4,800 acres, with miles of trails, beaches, and river access, offer ample opportunities for exploration in this varied and refreshing landscape. The beach, a mile from the highway at its closest point, is rarely crowded. A walk along the river or out to the coast can easily fill an afternoon, and more ambitious hikers will appreciate the panoramic views of Big Sur afforded by the East Molera Trail as it climbs into the nearby mountains. Horseback riding is a popular activity here, and a private stable leads guided rides through the state park, including sunset rides on the bluffs above the coast.

Andrew Molera State Park has few facilities other than an expansive, primitive trail camp, located ⅓ mile from the parking lot. The camp can accommodate over 400 people and is a well-known overnight stop for cyclists. Andrew Molera State Park is just over 20 miles south of Carmel on Highway 1. (408) 667-2315.

(Top): Evening descends on Garrapata State Beach.
(Above): Horseback riders, Andrew Molera State Park.

between December and May. An hour or two will suffice for walking a trail and observing some of the reserve's animals, birds, and plant life, but an entire day at Point Lobos can be a memorable experience and allows time for a picnic, to explore tide pools at Weston Beach, to chat with volunteer naturalists, and to visit the information center in Whalers Cabin. A variety of guided tours are offered on a regular basis, and many people, attracted by the reserve's uncrowded, unspoiled atmosphere and varied wildlife, return time and again to reacquaint themselves with this exceptional environment.

When planning a park visit, comfortable walking shoes and a pair of binoculars are highly recommended. There are picnic tables and restrooms, but no camping. Dogs are not permitted. Reserve hours are from 9 a.m. to 5 p.m. daily, with extended evening hours in summer. A limited number of guests are allowed to enter the reserve at one time, so on busy days there may be a wait at the entrance station. Point Lobos State Reserve is three miles south of Carmel on Highway 1. (408) 624-4909.

Garrapata State Park

Largely undeveloped, Garrapata State Park features over four miles of Big Sur coastline at Soberanes Point along with 2,879 acres of adjoining countryside.

Sea lions, harbor seals, and sea otters frequent the coastal waters, and California gray whales pass close by on their yearly migration. Park rangers conduct whale-watching tours at Garrapata during January. Two moderately rigorous trails connect the coast with the rugged hills to the east, passing through cactus stands and redwood groves, and affording tremendous ocean views. The park has no entrance station or designated parking lot. Roadside turnouts along the highway provide access to the beach at several points. Garrapata State Park is 10 miles south of Carmel on Highway 1. (408) 667-2315.

Point Sur State Historic Park

The lighthouse and fog signal at Point Sur, still in service today under the management of the U.S. Coast Guard, were established in 1889 for the safety of seagoing vessels moving up and down the Big Sur coast. Four lighthouse keepers and their families lived a quiet life at Point Sur, having little contact with the outside world. The last keeper departed in 1974 when the light station was automated. The homes, workshops, and lighthouse of this turn-of-the-century outpost may be toured each Sunday on a limited basis. Point Sur State Historic Park is clearly visible on the bluff at Point Sur. The park entrance is about 15 miles south of Carmel along High-

(Top): A horned nudibranch. (Bottom): Visitor at tidepools, Año Nuevo State Reserve.

Exploring California's Tide Pools and Underwater Parks

The coastal waters of California draw millions of visitors every year who come for scuba diving, snorkeling, and tide pool exploration. Just offshore are underwater wonderlands, teeming with myriad forms of marine life that delight divers with their bright colors, unusual shapes, or intriguing behavior. Closer to shore are intertidal zones where pools form at low tide, and, like small aquariums, give visitors a chance to view marine life up close. Not long ago, unrestricted collecting and harvesting of sea life led to a dangerous reduction in invertebrate populations in near-shore and intertidal waters, but a growing awareness of this threat has resulted in programs designed to preserve these resources for the enjoyment of future generations.

Tide Pools

Tide pools are generally found along gently sloping, rocky stretches of shore where submerged reefs and rocks are exposed when the tide is out. During the lowest tides, a rich variety of intertidal marine life is revealed, including worms, algae, sponges, seaweeds, sea stars (starfish), mollusks, sea anemones, crabs, and small fish. Good tide pool areas within the state park system include Patrick's Point and Salt Point in Northern California, Asilomar, Point Lobos, San Simeon, and Montaña de Oro along the central coast, and at Refugio, Carpinteria, Leo Carrillo, Point Dume, Royal Palms, and Cardiff in Southern California. A pocket field guide on the local marine flora and fauna will greatly enhance your visit to the tidepools. Tide charts, available at sporting goods stores, can be consulted to determine the best time for a visit. From November through March, the best tide pools are uncovered in the afternoon; April through July are the best months for early morning tide pool viewing.

Wherever you choose to observe tide pools, please check with park staff for directions and regulations. Remember, no life forms or shells may be gathered from tide pools other than a limited number of species that may be taken in season by licensed individuals. Respect tide pool creatures by walking carefully and replacing every stone or shell to its original position. And be conscious of safety; don't scale cliffs that are unsafe, watch your step on slippery rocks, keep an eye on the movement of the tides, and be aware that from time to time "sleeper" waves rush onto the shore, far beyond the normal tide line.

Underwater Parks

California's efforts to provide coastal recreational opportunities and preserve endangered species and marine habitats have led to the establishment of a number of underwater parks. Since the nation's first underwater reserve was established at Point Lobos State Reserve in 1960, many other underwater areas around the world have been similarly protected. Over 6,000 acres of underwater lands have been added to California state parks and recreation areas, including acreage at MacKerricher, Russian Gulch, Van Damme, Manchester, Salt Point, Fort Ross, Point Lobos, Julia Pfeiffer Burns, Crystal Cove, and Doheny. These underwater parks provide California's 400,000 divers with rare opportunities to explore unique marine communities that are either endangered or especially representative of an area. In addition to their value as recreational and biological resources, many underwater areas also contain valuable archaeological resources including the remains of sunken vessels. As with tide pools, preservation of the underwater parks depends on the visitors' respect for the historical artifacts and sea life found there.

Divers can view an amazing array of life in the kelp forests and rocky inlets along the coast. Some are fortunate enough to get a close look at seals, sea lions, and sea otters. Only certified divers are allowed to use California's underwater parks and reserves. The number of divers must be limited in order to minimize human impact on the underwater environment. Nondiving visitors needn't feel left out, however; most underwater parks have adjacent and easily accessible tide pool areas, and an increasing number of seaside and underwater parks feature interpretive displays, videos, programs, and literature that contribute to the enjoyment of this unique environment.

Coast redwoods along the Big Sur River.

Pfeiffer Big Sur State Park

Comfortable year-round camping among tall redwoods attracts a continuous stream of visitors to Pfeiffer Big Sur State Park, where hiking trails, swimming holes, lush riverbanks, and more than 800 acres of redwood, mixed conifer, and oak forest offer a variety of activities for people of all ages. Trails give access to the river, meadows, and forest groves of the valley, and also to Pfeiffer Falls, Big Sur Gorge, and overlooks that provide panoramic views of the Pacific Ocean and Big Sur Valley. The park is a major trailhead for trips into the Ventana Wilderness.

Camping accommodations are extensive; over 200 family sites (no hookups) are situated along a two-mile section of the Big Sur River, with convenient restrooms, showers, and laundry tubs. There are also two 50-person group sites, a bike-in camp for 30 people, a spacious playing field, and facilities for family or group picnics. The Big Sur Lodge operates room and cabin accommodations and a swimming pool for private guests. Stores, a restaurant, laundromat, and information center are located near the entrance to the park. The nearest beaches are Pfeiffer Beach off Sycamore Canyon Rd. one mile south of the park, and at Andrew Molera State Park several miles up the coast. Pfeiffer Big Sur State Park is 26 miles south of Carmel on Highway 1. (408) 667-2315.

Julia Pfeiffer Burns State Park

Located along one of the most rugged sections of the Big Sur coast, Julia Pfeiffer Burns State Park features a beautiful little cove surrounded by high bluffs and a 50-foot-high waterfall that drops directly into the ocean. The cove and waterfall can be viewed from Overlook Trail, which crosses under Highway 1 to a parking area in the mouth of McWay Canyon.

The park also includes 1,800 acres of upland forest and ridge country and a 1,680-acre underwater reserve. Two miles north of the main entrance, Partington Cove has unparalleled scuba diving, but only experienced divers should enter these treacherous waters. Tan Bark Trail switchbacks up from Partington Cove to a ridgetop with spectacular views of the coast. An eight-mile-long loop trail enables hikers to travel through the high country between Partington and McWay canyons. Julia Pfeiffer Burns State Park is on Highway 1, 12 miles south of Pfeiffer Big Sur. (408) 667-2315.

San Luis Obispo County

Hearst San Simeon State Historical Monument

La Cuesta Encantada, the "Enchanted Hill" high above the ocean at San Simeon, was the creation of two extraordinary individuals, William Randolph Hearst and architect Julia Morgan. Their collaboration, which began in 1919 and continued for nearly 30 years, transformed an informal hilltop camp-

site into the world-famous Hearst Castle—a magnificent 130-room main house plus guesthouses, pools, and 130 acres of cultivated gardens. The mansion itself, "La Casa Grande," is a grand setting for Hearst's collection of European antiques and art pieces. It was also a most fitting site for hosting the many influential guests who stayed at Hearst's 250,000-acre San Simeon ranch. Guests included President Calvin Coolidge, Winston Churchill, George Bernard Shaw, Charles Lindbergh, Charlie Chaplin, and a diverse array of luminaries from the show business and publishing industries.

A million tourists a year now visit Hearst San Simeon State Historical Monument. Daily tours of the buildings and grounds are conducted year-round except on holidays, and it is highly recommended that tours be reserved several weeks in advance. A brochure describing four different tour formats is available; first-time visitors usually prefer Tour 1, which provides the best introduction to the monument. A modern visitor center houses an information desk, gift shop, snack bar, and exhibit room. There are a few picnic tables near the parking area, but no overnight facilities are available. Scheduled tours begin at the visitor center, and buses transport visitors five miles up the hill to Hearst's palatial residence. The entrance to Hearst San Simeon State Historical Monument is about an hour's drive north of Morro Bay along Highway 1. (805) 927-2000.

William Randolph Hearst Memorial State Beach

A lovely little cove is the backdrop for this small park's picnic areas and fishing pier. The cove is protected from rough seas and winds, making it an ideal spot for swimming and wading. A concessionaire on the pier sells fishing licenses, rents fishing equipment, and operates a sports fishing boat. The beach is entered from Highway 1, directly opposite the visitor center in Hearst San Simeon State Historical Monument. (805) 927-2020.

San Simeon State Beach

Two miles of varied shoreline between Cambria and San Simeon are the setting for San Simeon State Beach. Three prime day-use areas are located on Moonstone Beach Dr.—Santa Rosa Creek, Leffingwell Landing, and Vista Point—all of which provide excellent opportunities for surf and rock fishing, tide pool exploration, and wandering among the driftwood in sandy coves. The main park entrance north of San Simeon Creek serves two campgrounds. San Simeon Creek campground has 134 improved sites as well as hike-and-bike camping. Trailers and campers up to 35 feet are allowed, and there is a sanitation station near the park entrance. Washburn primitive campground, located on a nearby hill, has 70 sites for trailers up to 21 feet and motor homes to 31 feet. On the south side of San Simeon Creek is the Washburn day-use area, which also serves as an overflow for at least 70 campers.

There are ample opportunities for beachcombing or surf fishing, and bird watching is particularly good since the shore, the creek, a marsh, and a number of open fields are all in close proximity. The campground at San Simeon State Beach is open all year and is located on Highway 1. It is the nearest state camping facility for tourists heading for Hearst San Simeon State Historical Monument, five miles to the north. (805) 927-2020.

Cayucos State Beach

Five miles north of Morro Bay, the small town of Cayucos is dominated by its centrally located fishing pier, adjacent picnic facilities, and sandy beach. The pier is lit for night fishing; equip-ment rentals, boating services, and snack bars are nearby, and a lifeguard is on duty during the summer. Cayucos State Beach, located at the foot of Cayucos Dr., is operated by the County of San Luis Obispo. (805) 549-5200.

Morro Strand State Beach

Along Estero Bay, a 3-mile section of sandy shoreline connects the northern and southern entrances to Morro Strand State Beach. Previously known as Atascadero State Beach, Morro Strand's seaside camping is popular with fishermen and anyone with a hankering for salt air and miles of open beach. The spacious sands invite beachgoers to jog, fly kites, or build sandcastles, and the sea is very popular with wind surfers.

To the north, on the outskirts of Cayucos, there is a parking area and set of restrooms at Pacific Ave. and 24th St. To the south, a paved RV camping area behind low dunes provides 104 sites suitable for trailers and campers up to 24 feet in length, with nearby restrooms and cold showers for a rinse after a day at the beach. Off Highway 1 in Morro Bay, the campground is reached by the Yerba Buena exit just north of town. Three miles up the highway, signs mark the exit for 24th St. and the northern access to Morro Strand State Beach. (805) 772-2560.

(Top left): Hearst Castle. (Above): Sea gulls at San Simeon State Beach.

Morro Bay State Park

Directly south of the pleasant seaside community of Morro Bay, this 1,913-acre park provides townspeople and tourists alike with a picturesque, 18-hole public golf course, a colorful marina, and a noteworthy natural history museum—all amid a unique setting where a long, narrow sandspit creates a calm bay and protected boat harbor. Visitors to Morro Bay State Park enjoy golfing, boating, fishing, bird watching, beach walks, guided nature walks and campfire programs, and the marina's cafe and boat/bike rentals, as well as the town's harbor, seafood restaurants, shops, and beaches. On the bay's northeast edge is a pristine saltwater marsh that supports a thriving bird population. The Muse-

(Above): Coast Live Oaks, Los Osos Oaks Reserve. (Top): Surf splashes onto sedimentary rock at Montaña de Oro State Park. (Opposite): The old bell tower, La Purísima Mission.

um of Natural History is perched on a rise overlooking the bay and its most prominent landmark, Morro Rock.

The campground is nicely situated in a grove of trees between the marina and the golf course, with 135 developed sites, perfect for tent camping, trailers, and campers up to 31 feet. Twenty of these sites have RV hookups, and a sanitation station is provided. Hike-and-bike camping and group sites are also available. Campground reservations are a must in summer and are recommended for any weekend during the year. To reach Morro Bay State Park from Highway 1, take the Morro Bay Blvd. exit ½ mile west to the park entrance. From the center of town, Morro Bay State Park is a short drive south on Main St. (805) 772-2560.

Montaña de Oro State Park

The prominent dunes on the south side of Morro Bay's sandspit mark the northern boundary of Montaña de Oro State Park. Encompassing 8,066 acres of untamed coastline and coastal uplands, the park has over 3½ miles of shoreline and extends eastward into rough, hilly terrain. Naturalists, back-packers, and equestrians appreciate the solitude and freedom they find along the trails that wind through these lonesome hills. The shore south of the sandspit is predominantly rugged and rocky, sculpted for millenia by crashing waves and sea spray. Tide pools and sandy coves are tucked away below the cliffs and often inaccessible. A network of pathways on the blufftops opens up the coastline for walking, jogging, and taking it all in.

Spooners Cove, across from the campground, is the primary beach access. The family campground is 2½ miles beyond the park entrance. Situated above the banks of a small creek, this primitive camp is clean, quiet, and grassy, and has plenty of shade trees. Additional camping is available in trail camps in the backcountry, and a horse camp is located near the park entrance. Montaña de Oro State Park is six miles southwest of Morro Bay, via South Bay Blvd., Los Osos Valley Rd., and Pecho Rd. Alternatively, a freeway exit off U. S. Highway 101 just north of Pismo Beach leads to Los Osos Valley Rd. and on to Montaña de Oro. (805) 772-2560 or 528-0513.

Los Osos Oaks State Reserve

Within this 85-acre reserve, trails wander through stands of heavily gnarled, 700-year-old oaks and more open areas with smaller, moss-covered oak trees and coastal vegetation. There is a parking area but no facilities. The reserve is located in Los Osos, on Los Osos Valley Rd., seven miles south of its junction with South Bay Blvd. (805) 528-0513.

Pismo State Beach

A broad expanse of sand and tree-lined dunes brings visitors to Pismo State Beach year after year for surf fishing, sunbathing, beach play, bird watching, horseback riding, or long walks among the dunes. Digging for the famed Pismo clam has long been a main attraction here, although legal-sized clams are rare these days. Clamming regulations and limits are posted and strictly enforced. Two campgrounds, a mile apart, are situated near the beach and the Pismo Beach Golf Course. The North Beach Campground, with 103 improved sites, is grassy, open, and well protected from stiff ocean breezes by a narrow strip of sand dunes. To the south, adjacent to a creek and small

lagoon, Oceano Campground has over 80 campsites—31 of which have hook-ups and hot showers. Hike-and-bike camping is also available. Pismo State Beach is located on Highway 1, just two miles south of the town of Pismo Beach. (805) 489-8655.

Pismo Dunes State Vehicular Recreation Area

Pismo Dunes State Vehicular Recreation Area opens some 1,800 acres of sand dunes and beach to off-highway and "street-legal" vehicles throughout the year. Enthusiasts show up in every type of off-highway rig. The area also offers swimming, fishing, surf fishing, and hiking. Camping is permitted on the beach and in the sand dune area that is open to off-highway vehicles. Four-wheel drive is recommended. Posted vehicle and safety regulations must be followed.

The recreation area includes a relatively fragile dune environment to the south that is off-limits to vehicles but open to foot traffic and horseback riding. Hikers and equestrians can enter this protected area from a parking lot at the south end of the park near Oso Flaco Lake. Pismo Dunes State Vehicular Recreation Area is located in Oceano, three miles south of Pismo Beach. (805) 549-3433.

Northern Santa Barbara County

Point Sal State Beach

Seals and sea birds flock to Point Sal, but this isolated central coast beach is rarely crowded with people. Located at the end of a dirt road, Point Sal State Beach offers solitude by the wild, open sea. The current here is too treacherous for swimming, but the waters are a favorite site for surf fishing. Point Sal is nine miles southwest of Guadalupe via Highway 1 and Brown Rd. The four-mile, unpaved section of Brown Rd. may be impassable in winter. (805) 733-3713.

La Purísima Mission State Historic Park

One of the most successful communities of the California mission system was Misión la Purísima Concepción de María Santísima, founded in 1787.

The fertile lands it occupied, combined with the cooperation of the Chumash Indians and local ranchers, brought its inhabitants a relatively peaceful and prosperous life. The original site was damaged beyond repair in 1812 by an earthquake and heavy rains, but the mission was moved across the Santa Ynez River Valley to its present site and rebuilt. After the mission system was closed down, La Purísima continued to serve for a time as a parish church, but eventually it was abandoned and fell into ruin.

In the 1930s the WPA and CCC organizations spent seven years restoring and reconstructing the adobe buildings of La Purísima. The church, chapel, padre's living quarters, workshops, infirmary buildings, and a variety of living quarters have all been rebuilt. Today these buildings and their undisturbed, natural setting in *Cañada de los Berros* make this the largest, most complete, and most authentic mission restoration project in the American West. The park's early-California atmosphere has been further enhanced by the addition of livestock and plants that were utilized by the original settlers. La Purísima includes a visitor center, museum, picnic area, and a self-guiding tour. Plan to spend at least two hours. La Purísima Mission State Historic Park is three miles from Lompoc along Highway 246 and Purisima Rd. (805) 733-3713.

(Top): Yearling northern elephant seal at Año Nuevo State Reserve. (Above): Playful sea otters.

Sea Mammals of California

Since ancient times, people have been fascinated by sea mammals. The Chumash Indians believed that dolphins were humans who had fallen into the sea, and called them the "brothers of mankind." Today many people are familiar with whales, dolphins, and seals from television programs and zoos, but few have ever had the opportunity to observe these captivating creatures in their natural habitat. Many California state parks, beaches, and reserves offer just such opportunities for observation. Sea mammals found along the California coast fall into three groups: cetaceans (whales, dolphins, and porpoises), pinnipeds (seals and sea lions), and, in a class of their own, sea otters.

One of the reasons people find sea mammals so intriguing is that, unlike most other sea animals, they resemble humans in many ways: they breathe air, bear live offspring, and some have complex social structures; they are intelligent and playful, and their grace and agility in the water is the envy of many. Dolphins, porpoises, and whales communicate with each other in sophisticated ways; in close encounters with humans they often appear curious and friendly. It is a sad irony that many species of California's sea mammals were once hunted to the brink of extinction. Fortunately, these animals are now protected under the Marine Mammal Protection Act. Many, including the sea otter and some whale species, are also protected under the Endangered Species Act.

Seals and sea lions are found along the entire length of the California coast. Herds of California sea lions, the shiny black "trained seals" at zoos and marine parks, feed and breed at certain areas, such as Lighthouse Point in Santa Cruz and at Año Nuevo and Point Lobos state reserves on the central coast. They can be seen on rocky promontories or beaches, and their energetic barking can be heard from quite a distance. The Steller sea lion, larger than its cousins and yellow-brown in color, has one of its main colonies at Año Nuevo State Reserve. The harbor seal, recognized by its spotted coat and innocent, puppy-like face, is relatively small for a pinniped, weighing 150 to 200 pounds. It frequents quiet harbors, inland bays, and river mouths, as well as exposed outer coasts such as Point Lobos and San Simeon. In spring, harbor seals and their pups can be seen along the shore at Point Lobos State Reserve. The northern elephant seal is the largest seal of all, with males sometimes exceeding 16 feet in length and two tons in weight. Even more astounding than its size is the male's distinctive, trunk-like snout. The only mainland colony of northern elephant seals in North America is located at Año Nuevo State Reserve, where daily guided walks from December to April provide access to the seaside trails opposite their island breeding area.

Sea otters are well known for their joyful antics and clever use of rocks as tools for breaking open shellfish. Not long ago, though, sea otters were hunted relentlessly for their valuable pelts. Today, there are fewer than 2,000 sea otters along the California coast and most are found from Monterey to San Luis Obispo, where otter-watching is a popular pastime.

At once frolicsome and graceful, dolphins and porpoises can sometimes be seen from shore, especially between August and January. The common dolphin, the Pacific white-sided dolphin, and the harbor porpoise are the three most commonly sighted species. The bottle-nosed dolphin is much larger than the more commonly sighted species and is recognized by its prominent dorsal fin. A friendly sea mammal that takes well to captivity, the bottle-nosed dolphin also appears to have a sophisticated system of communication. The largest of the dolphins is the killer whale, or orca. Often hunting in groups, killer whales attack other dolphins, seals, and even other whales.

Of the whales that visit the state's coastal waters, the California gray whale is the one most commonly spotted from shore. Its 13,000-mile annual migration—from the Bering Sea to Baja California and back— closely follows the Pacific coastline, making these marine giants visible from land. The months to sight these whales are December through April, with January and March being particularly good for whale-watching. Many parks and reserves offer good look-out points, or even guided walks for observing the California gray whale. Other whales that can be seen off the coast include the blue whale and the humpback whale.

CHAPTER FOUR

Central California Inland

From the interior foothills of the Coast Range on the west, to Sacramento and Lake Tahoe on the north, to the desert areas of Southern California, California's central inland landscape includes the whole San Joaquin Valley and much of the Sierra Nevada. Rising gently from its oak- and pine-forested foothills, the Sierra Nevada—John Muir's "Range of Light"—culminates in a snow-covered crest that defines the east side of central California. This wall of dramatic peaks dominates inland California's topography and extends its influence both east and west.

In the rain shadow created by the steep eastern escarpment of the Sierra Nevada are two of California's premier state parks. Near Lee Vining, small creeks tumble along steep ravines towards Mono Lake, a vibrant blue gem completely surrounded by sagebrush and volcanic craters. Mono Lake Tufa State Reserve protects the fascinating shoreline of this unique body of water. Nearby, barren desert hills encircle the ghostly remains of Bodie, the once-thriving gold town that is now preserved within Bodie State Historic Park.

Several parks along the western slope of the Sierra Nevada tell the story of human settlement and exploration in this vast area. Until the Gold Rush brought fortune seekers swarming into the Mother Lode, only California Indians inhabited the Sierra foothills, establishing winter camps in the foothills and moving into the higher eleva-

tions in summer to trade with Indian groups from east of the mountains. Parks such as Indian Grinding Rock and Wassama Round House preserve important California Indian food-gathering and ceremonial centers. But Indian encampments dwindled as gold towns like Columbia attracted a growing stream of prospectors, miners, loggers, merchants, and recreational travelers. Pressing deeper into the range, these people gradually discovered the Sierra's alpine meadows, granite outcrops, and other scenic attractions, and paved the way for modern-day visitors to Yosemite—the first state park in the California system, now a national park—and to the giant Sequoias at today's Calaveras Big Trees State Park. By 1897 the Mother Lode country was even serviced by a railroad—the Sierra Railway Company—whose steam locomotives are now housed at Railtown 1897 State Historic Park. In the 20th century, several large reservoirs including Turlock and Millerton lakes, were built to supply water to the San Joaquin Valley's rich agricultural land. Today, these reservoirs are part of the State Park System and provide important recreational opportunities for swimmers, waterskiers, and fishermen.

Most meltwater from the Sierra's dense snowpack travels west in a maze of rivers that flow north through the San Joaquin Valley to merge with the south and westbound waters of the Sacramento River and San Joaquin Delta. The delta wetlands, as exemplified by Franks Tract and Brannan

Island state recreation areas, are bursting with wildlife—fish, aquatic and field birds, small animals—and the numerous waterways are a haven for fishermen, waterskiers, swimmers, and naturalists.

The Diablo Range, where flora and fauna of both northern and southern California can be found, is easily accessible from the San Francisco Bay Area and northern San Joaquin Valley. Recreational opportunities abound, whether it be hiking in the woodlands of Mt. Diablo or Henry Coe state parks, fishing or water sports at Bethany and Lake Del Valle state recreation areas, or the challenging trails at Carnegie State Vehicular Recreation Area.

The San Joaquin Valley, a vast and fertile basin cradled between the Sierra Nevada and Coast ranges, is California's agricultural heartland. Here, state parks along the banks of the San Joaquin, Merced, Tuolumne, and Stanislaus rivers help preserve riparian habitats that are home to many species of birds, animals, and plants. Lined with shady canopies of valley oak, the rivers are a cool retreat in summer with good swimming and picnicking, while fishing, boating, and hiking are enjoyed any time of the year. These rivers are accessible at state parks and recreation areas such as McConnell, Fremont Ford, George J. Hatfield, Durham Ferry, and Caswell Memorial. In the southern end of the valley are two of California's most unusual parks, Tule Elk State Reserve and Allensworth State Historic Park.

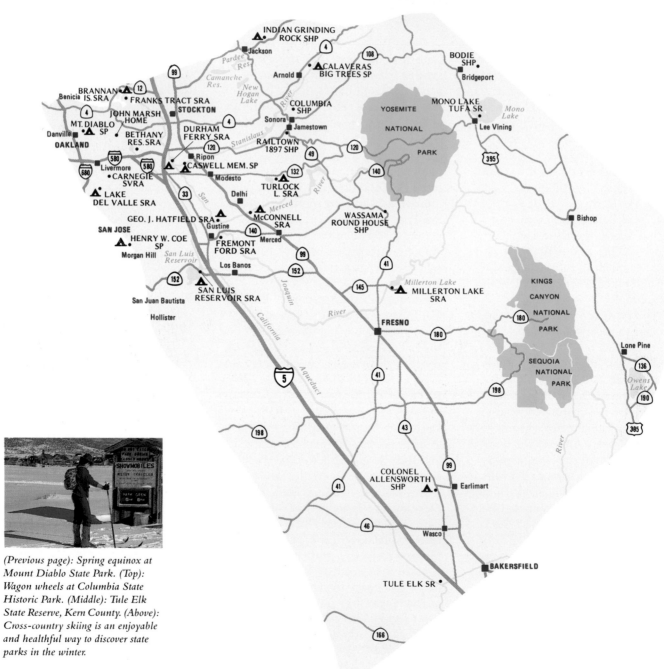

(Previous page): Spring equinox at Mount Diablo State Park. (Top): Wagon wheels at Columbia State Historic Park. (Middle): Tule Elk State Reserve, Kern County. (Above): Cross-country skiing is an enjoyable and healthful way to discover state parks in the winter.

Eastern Sierra Nevada

Bodie State Historic Park

In the late 1850s, Waterman S. Body (William Bodey) discovered small amounts of gold in the windswept hills just north of Mono Lake. But the town that bears his name amounted to little until 1877, when the Standard Company struck pay dirt, and a gold rush of giant proportions transformed Bodie from a small hamlet of 20 citizens to a boomtown of several thousand miners, storekeepers, hotel operators, teamsters, gamblers, and others. With its Chinatown, red light district, shootings, rich strikes, and hard luck, Bodie came to epitomize the wide-open, fast-moving, gold-rush West. Now an authentic ghost town, Bodie has been preserved in a state of "arrested decay" since 1962, allowing visitors to observe authentic remnants of Bodie's heydey unchanged by modern intrusions.

One could easily spend an entire day wandering the streets of Bodie. Interiors remain as they were left and stocked with goods. Storefronts and tucked-away windows invite visitors to peek into the past and imagine the former residents, storekeepers, and gamblers busy at their daily tasks. An informative self-guiding brochure is available, and from Memorial Day through Labor Day there are history talks and weekend tours through the Standard Mill. The Miners' Union Hall has been set aside as a museum, and a good selection of reading material on Bodie, mining history, and eastern California history is available at the park office. There are eight picnic sites but no overnight accommodations. Winter weather can be bitterly cold, so between October and May travelers are advised to bring warm coats, hats, and gloves, along with their cameras and extra film.

Six miles south of Bridgeport along U.S. Highway 395, the Bodie Rd. turn-off leads 13 miles to Bodie. There is also an approach from Highway 167 on Mono Lake's north shore. Both roads are subject to winter closure due to snow. (619) 647-6445.

Mono Lake Tufa State Reserve

Covering 60 square miles, Mono Lake is flanked by towering, snow-covered peaks to the west, volcanic craters to

the north and south, and the vast reaches of the Great Basin to the east. It is a setting with few equals, and has become a regular destination for those with a passion for photography, geology, or bird watching. At first glance this landscape is seemingly barren, but a closer inspection of Mono Lake reveals an environment that teems with life. With no outlet, Mono is a salty, alkaline lake that has developed a unique ecosystem that supports hundreds of thousands of migrating and nesting birds each year. The brine fly and a species of brine shrimp found only in Mono Lake are the major food supply for these birds.

For thousands of years, calcium-rich water from submerged hot springs has mixed with carbonates in the salty lake water to build up unusual underwater spires known as tufa towers. Since 1941, when the City of Los Angeles began diverting water from four of the seven streams that empty into Mono Lake, the lake level has dropped significantly, exposing the tufa to view. At the South Tufa Area, guided naturalist tours are given on a regular basis. A short but fairly steep trail near the South Tufa Area ascends to the top of Panum Crater for a firsthand view of one of Mono's volcanoes. On the north shore, hikers can climb up to Black Point, where an underwater volcano has left tufa-lined fissures several feet wide and 50 feet deep. A boardwalk trail, popular with birders, begins at Mono Lake County Park, providing access to a marsh, tufa towers, and the lake's shoreline.

(Top): Main Street, Bodie State Historic Park.
(Above): Tufa towers at Mono Lake.

Western Sierra Nevada

Indian Grinding Rock State Historic Park

In the Mother Lode country's mixed oak and pine woodlands, this small, quiet park is dedicated to the Miwok Indians who established winter camps in the vicinity before the Gold Rush. The park's peaceful atmosphere helps visitors conjure up images of the Miwok way of life before the coming of white settlers and gold-seekers. Used for centuries by the Indians in preparing their dietary staple of acorn meal, a broad, low limestone outcrop in the middle of the property displays over a thousand mortar cups, or *chaw'se,* worn into its surface.

The park's excellent Chaw'se Regional Indian Museum is operated by an active and enthusiastic staff, who, with the help of numerous volunteers, give varied programs and demonstrations of traditional Miwok crafts. The grounds are dotted with barkhouses— teepee-shaped sleeping structures of pine logs and cedar bark. An impressive round house, the traditional structure that served as the social and ceremonial heart of many California Indian communities, is located near the grinding rock. Today, the grounds and round house at Indian Grinding Rock are still used for joint gatherings of many different tribes.

Indian Grinding Rock has year-round camping, with 21 family campsites and a special walk-in environmental campground with six barkhouse shelters. Reservations are recommended. Day-use facilities include picnic sites, a self-guided tour, and the museum, which is sometimes closed on Thursdays and Fridays. Highway 88 runs east from Jackson to the town of Pine Grove, where a marked turnoff and one-mile drive on Pine Grove-Volcano Rd. leads to Indian Grinding Rock State Historic Park. (209) 296-7488.

Calaveras Big Trees State Park

Growing up to 33 feet in diameter and 325 feet in height, giant sequoias are the largest and one of the tallest living things in the world. They are survivors from those prehistoric times, 100 million years ago and more, when vast forests of redwoods occurred

in many parts of the northern hemisphere and giant reptiles—dinosaurs— roamed the earth.

In 1853, a bear hunter named A. T. Dowd chased a wounded grizzly into the North Grove of what is now Calaveras Big Trees State Park. Stunned by the sight of a tree a hundred feet in circumference, Dowd let the bear escape and spent the rest of the day exploring before returning to town to tell about his amazing discovery. Dowd was not the first person to see the big trees—the trees had long been sacred to the Indians, and over the years other people had "discovered" them—but it was Dowd whose story helped convince a skeptical public that such large and otherwise impressive trees really did exist. Much to his disgust, the grove was soon being exploited in a fashion typical of the rather insensitive entrepreneurship of the 19th century. Among other things, Dowd's "Discovery Tree" was cut down and shipped East for exhibition. A bowling alley and covered pavilion were built atop the remaining portions of its fallen trunk. Still other atrocities followed.

At Mono Lake State Reserve visitors enjoy swimming, canoeing and kayaking, astronomy programs, cycling, and even cross-country skiing. During winter be prepared for cold weather and snow. Both state and federal park personnel have offices in Lee Vining, and the Mono Lake Committee operates an excellent visitor center. There are no campgrounds at the lake, but camping is permitted on federal land away from the shoreline, and private and public campgrounds with full facilities are located within 15 miles. Mono Lake is adjacent to Lee Vining, and can be reached by travelling east through Yosemite National Park on Highway 120, or north from Bishop or south from Bridgeport via U.S. Highway 395. (619) 647-6331.

(Bottom left): Pacific dogwood, North Grove, Calaveras Big Trees State Park. (Top left): Bedrock mortars, Indian Grinding Rock State Historic Park. (Above): Wassama Roundhouse, Indian Grinding Rock State Historic Park. (Opposite): Columbia State Historic Park.

Today the grove has regained much of its original solemnity. A nature trail guides visitors on an easy stroll through the grove, and you even walk right up onto the stump of the Discovery Tree or play peek-a-boo in a hollow log big enough to ride through on horseback. The South Grove of Calaveras Big Trees is located about nine miles to the south and is accessible only by a short walk. It has been left in its wild and natural condition. Other areas of the 6,000-acre park offer picnicking, wading, fishing, hiking, and a magnificent vista of the Sierra Nevada. For campers, there are 129 developed campsites, with the main campground located within an easy walk of the North Grove. The park is four miles northeast of Arnold, on Highway 4. (209) 795-2334.

Columbia State Historic Park

When rich gold-bearing gravel was discovered here in 1850, the shanty-town of Hildreth's Diggings rapidly swelled into the swarming metropolis of Columbia. With a population of 6,000, it became for a time the second-largest city in California. What today would amount to more than a billion dollars of gold was mined from these foothills over a period of 20 years, making Columbia the "Queen of the Southern Mines." The mines, however, were exhausted by the 1870s, and the town dwindled to a small though permanent community.

Since Columbia became a state historic park in 1945, the old business district has been preserved and restored. Visitors step into the spirited 1850s, and, as in years past, try their hand at panning for gold, ride the stagecoach, and share in the fun at the local theater. A self-guided tour covering 12 square blocks describes museum displays and points of interest, and the mile-long Karen Bakerville Smith Memorial Nature Trail introduces guests to the natural history of Columbia's environs. Now a booming tourist town, Columbia's entertainment activities include square dancing, swimming, fishing, melodramas, and special events. There are restaurants, snack shops, saloons, a candy store, a blacksmith shop, souvenir shops, a bakery, a hotel, and a picnic area in Columbia. Private camp-grounds with trailer hookups are located nearby. Open year-round, except Thanksgiving and Christmas, Columbia State Historic Park is located three miles north of Sonora on Highway 49. (209) 532-4301 or 532-0150.

Railtown 1897 State Historic Park

In 1897, a shortline railroad run by the Sierra Railway Company began moving passengers and freight through the Mother Lode country. The line's Jamestown station is now Railtown 1897 State Historic Park, the home of many old steam locomotives that were replaced by diesel engines in the 1950s. From the end of May through the summer, Railtown's locomotives take visitors on both short rides and longer excursions. Tours of the roundhouse and blacksmith shop are offered on weekends. There is also a picnic area, restaurant, gift shop, and slide program. Railtown 1897 is located in Jamestown, three miles south of Sonora on Highway 49. (209) 984-3953.

Wassama Roundhouse State Historic Park

This small park is located in the Sierra foothills and is used by local Native Americans for dances and other ceremonies. The park is operated by the Wassama Association and is open to the public on a schedule that varies with the season and other factors. Reservations can be made for guided tours, and a self-guiding tour brochure is available. A nominal admission fee is charged. Wassama Roundhouse State Historic Park is located on Highway 49, seven miles north of Oakhurst. (209) 822-2332.

Understanding the First Californians

As the state's population approaches 30 million people, it becomes increasingly difficult to imagine what California was like 250 years ago, when the only inhabitants were some 250,000 to 300,000 Indians living in self-sufficient communities throughout the state. The diverse heritage of the California Indians is an important link to this not-so-distant past, and reflects a wide range of customs and a variety of adaptations to regional environments. Coastal, valley, desert, and mountain groups exhibited similarities in dress and social life, yet many other cultural characteristics, such as building styles, ceremonies, tools, and religious beliefs, differed widely. Although their languages and customs were often dissimilar, the state's many Indian groups—hundreds of them—were not completely isolated from one another; goods and services were shared through a widespread network of trade.

California Indians reacted to explorers and settlers with mixed attitudes, but, whether friend or foe of the white man, they all eventually experienced a drastic reduction in population as western civilization took hold. Displacement, disease, violence, and forced relocation all contributed to the Indians' precipitous decline in population. Today, interest in the California Indian heritage is on the upswing; Indian people everywhere are strengthening their cultural ties, and helping to increase awareness and appreciation of a rich cultural fabric incorporating exacting survival skills, a universally relevant folklore, and a deep respect for nature.

Native Californians were distributed so widely over the state that many, if not most, state park facilities contain Indian sites of archaeological or historical import. Olompali State Historic Park, for example, was the location of the largest coastal Miwok village and a possible meeting place between Sir Francis Drake and the Miwok people. Pismo State Beach was an important location for coastal Indians who found a major food source in the famous Pismo clam. In Santa Barbara County, Chumash Painted Cave State Historic Park preserves an outstanding example of pictograph artwork. At Carpinteria State Beach, tarpits provided caulking material for the canoes of Chumash mariners, and the area that is now Point Mugu State Park was also an important center for this once-populous tribe.

More than ever, the California Department of Parks and Recreation is actively involved in helping Native Americans preserve and perpetuate their heritage by developing Indian sites as educational resources for all age groups. One of the ways parks promote better appreciation of this heritage is through outdoor, hands-on interpretive displays. Clear Lake State Park features an Indian nature trail that shows how Pomo Indians—

(Left): Bedrock mortars, Indian Grinding Rock State Historic Park. (Below): Miwok Indian dance ceremony, Indian Grinding Rock State Historic Park.

famous for their baskets—utilized the resources in their environment. Still undeveloped, Anderson Marsh State Historic Park is a place where visitors can inspect a ceremonial dance ring and reconstructed tule huts. Here, archaeologists have found traces of Native American culture dating back 10,000 years. At the remote Ahjumawi Lava Springs State Park, ancient fish traps are still maintained and used by the Ahjumawi people. At Tomales Bay, a ½-mile nature trail familiarizes visitors with the plants used by the Coast Miwok in their daily life. There is a ceremonial structure at Wassama Round House State Historic Park, an important Miwok site that is still used for Native American gatherings.

The park system's most thorough introductions to California Indian culture are found at the State Indian Museum in Sacramento and Indian Grinding Rock State Historic Park near Jackson in the Sierra foothills. The State Indian Museum houses displays and artifacts from various California Indian groups and hosts a number of events throughout the year. At Indian Grinding Rock, the Chaw'se Regional Indian Museum showcases Miwok culture and hosts public demonstrations and yearly gatherings. Park grounds include the immense rock where acorns were pounded to make flour, as well as a playing field and a ceremonial round-house. In addition to the family camping facilities, visitors can treat themselves to a stay in the environmental

campground, where authentic bark houses and the quietude of the Sierra foothills lend a sense of what early California life must have been like. Lake Perris State Recreation Area in Southern California is home to a new Regional Indian Museum.

Sizeable displays featuring a number of California tribes are on exhibit in museums throughout the State Park System. Notable among them are the ones at Fort Humboldt State Historic Park, Fort Ross State Historic Park, Sonoma State Historic Park, Morro Bay State Park, La Purísima Mission State Historic Park, Malibu Lagoon State Beach, Antelope Valley Indian Museum, San Pasqual Battlefield, Anza-Borrego Desert State Park, and Cuyamaca Rancho State Park.

Turlock Lake State Recreation Area. (Opposite): Mount Diablo State Park.

Turlock Lake State Recreation Area

Some distance from the population centers of the San Joaquin Valley yet close enough for a one-day trip, Turlock Lake State Recreation Area is situated in the rolling, oak-dotted terrain of the western Sierra Nevada foothills. The campground—with over 67 sites, flush toilets, and hot showers—is nestled in a narrow, woodsy pocket between the Tuolumne River and Turlock Lake. With the river and lake environments so close to each other, this recreation area offers the best of both worlds. Boating, waterskiing, swimming, and picnicking are all to be enjoyed at the lake, while the Tuolumne's banks invite fishing, canoeing, and bird watching. River users should be aware that the campground is not yet equipped with formal parking or picnic facilities; these are only available at the lakeshore or farther upstream, outside park boundaries. Turlock Lake is open year-round. The campground accommodates campers and trailers up to 18 feet long, but there are no hookups. To reach Turlock Lake, take Highway 132 east from Modesto approximately 20 miles to the Lake Rd. turnoff. (209) 874-2008.

Millerton Lake State Recreation Area

Friant Dam was constructed across the San Joaquin River here in 1944, creating Millerton Lake and inundating the small town of Millerton, which served for a while as the Fresno County seat. As the lake began to fill, the Millerton County Courthouse, built in 1867, was dismantled and reconstructed on higher ground near park headquarters, where it is now open to the public. The park includes over 40 miles of shoreline, a marina with supplies and boat rentals, protected swimming areas, boat launching ramps, improved family campgrounds, boat camping, trail camping, and two group campsites. Millerton Lake State Recreation Area is located 20 miles northeast of Fresno, via Highway 41 and Highway 145. (209) 822-2225 or 822-2332.

Sacramento-San Joaquin Delta

Brannan Island State Recreation Area

The maze of waterways through the Sacramento-San Joaquin Delta has formed countless islands and marshes, creating rich wildlife habitats and excellent recreational opportunities. At Brannan Island State Recreation Area, there is one family campground with over 100 campsites for tent or trailer camping (no hookups); several primitive group campsites are also available. There is a boat camp with 32 slips and adjacent walk-in campsites. Plenty of picnic spots and a swimming beach—with a lifeguard in the summer—make Brannan Island a great day-use destination. A large boat-launching ramp and roomy parking lot allow convenient river access, and the fishing is excellent, particularly when the "stripers"—striped bass—are running in spring and summer. Brannan Island is located along Highway 160, three miles south of Rio Vista. (916) 777-6671 or 777-5361. **See also Delta Meadows, page 41.**

Franks Tract State Recreation Area

This delta lake, accessible only by boat, is well-known for its good fishing, waterskiing, and waterfowl hunting. There are no developed facilities. Visitors to Franks Tract should check with the staff at Brannan Island State Recreation Area for information about boating and hunting regulations. (916) 777-6671.

Diablo Range

Mount Diablo State Park

Geographers have concluded that one can see more of the earth's surface from the summit of Mount Diablo than from any other point on earth with one exception—the top of 19,000-foot Mount Kilimanjaro in Africa. Long regarded as sacred by Indians, 3,849-foot Mount Diablo is not particularly high by California standards, but the panoramic view from its summit is impressive. On a good day its vistas take in approximately 40,000 square miles of central California, from the Golden Gate to the Sierra Nevada and from Lassen Peak to the vicinity of Mount Whitney. Diablo is also fascinating from a geological point of view in that one encounters successively older and older rocks as one climbs the mountain—exactly the reverse of the usual progression. The mountain was formed when a mass of underlying rock was gradually forced up through the earth's surface.

The 18,000-acre park is a hiker's paradise, with many miles of trail—some easy and some strenuous—ranging in length from less than a mile to 11 miles. Part of the "fire-ecology" trail that goes around the mountain near the summit is wheelchair accessible. There are 60 developed campsites, some of them with stunning views. Mount Diablo State Park is located on Diablo Rd., five miles east of Interstate 680 and the town of Danville. It can also be reached from Walnut Creek off Ygnacio Valley Rd. (415) 837-2525.

(Above): Buttercups and blue oaks, Henry W. Coe State Park. (Right): The Oak Forest Nature Trail, Caswell Memorial State Park. (Opposite): Merced River, McConnell State Recreation Area.

John Marsh Home

John Marsh was a Harvard graduate who spent several years in Wisconsin, New Mexico, and Sonora before arriving in California in 1836. He obtained a Mexican land grant at the foot of Mount Diablo in 1838 and settled permanently there. He prospered as a cattle rancher, and his letters to relatives in the United States helped spur American westward migration. His home near Brentwood, at the base of Mount Diablo in eastern Contra Costa County, is being stabilized, and the park is scheduled to open in 1990. (408) 649-2840.

Bethany Reservoir State Recreation Area

Set in the rolling hills of the northwestern San Joaquin Valley, Bethany is well-known to fishermen and windsurfers. Visitors here enjoy cycling along the California Aqueduct Bikeway, taking short hikes, picnicking, and boating; waterskiing and horseback riding are not permitted. Bethany Reservoir State Recreation Area is northeast of Livermore, seven miles off Interstate 580 at Grant Line Road exit. (415) 687-1800.

Carnegie State Vehicular Recreation Area

Off-road motorcyclists of all abilities are welcome to test their skills at this 1,500-acre site, which offers varied terrain and trails marked according to skill level. Along with regular day-use opportunities, Carnegie State Vehicular Recreation Area also has primitive camping available on Friday, Saturday, and pre-holiday nights. A ranger station, bike shop, and picnic area are also found here. The recreation area is on Telsa/Corral Hollow Rd., between Tracy and Livermore. (415) 447-9361 or 447-9027.

Lake Del Valle State Recreation Area

Lake Del Valle offers a variety of recreation, including fishing, boating, windsurfing, swimming, hiking, and horseback riding. The campground has RV hookups, a group site, and a backpacker camping area. Managed by the East Bay Regional Park District, the park is on Del Valle Rd., just a few miles south of Interstate 580 in Livermore. (415) 531-9300.

Henry W. Coe State Park

Located in the Diablo Range east of Morgan Hill and the Santa Clara Valley, this rugged 67,000-acre park was created in 1954 when Sada Sutcliffe Coe donated some 13,000 acres of land to the people of California for park purposes. Named in honor of Coe's father, Henry W. Coe State Park is a splendid place to get away from the rapid pace of city life. The variety of terrain and native plants—including deep canyons, beautiful manzanita groves, oak forests, and pine-covered ridges—makes the area excellent for plant and wild-life study.

A 125-mile trail system provides opportunities for hiking, horseback riding, and rigorous mountain biking; visitors can also enjoy a bit of fishing in the small reservoirs and abandoned cattle ponds of the old ranch. There are 20 primitive campsites near the park entrance, 10 hike-in group sites (water must be carried in), and several backpacker camps. The old ranch buildings are complemented by a small museum. Spring and fall are the most colorful seasons here, and the weather can be quite pleasant. In summer, extreme heat and dryness often necessitate restrictions on camping, cooking, and trail access, so be sure to call ahead to check on conditions. Please contact the ranger staff before entering the back country. From U.S. Highway 101 in Morgan Hill, take Dunne Ave. east; the park entrance is about 40 minutes by car from there. (408) 779-2728.

San Joaquin Valley

Durham Ferry State Recreation Area

A popular park for river fishing, Durham Ferry has an improved RV campground and picnic facilities in an open, grassy area adjacent to the San Joaquin River. The 176-acre recreation area has 1½ miles of river access (no boating or swimming), an equestrian area, and a nearby archery range. Operated by San Joaquin County, Durham Ferry State Recreation Area is about 10 miles west of Ripon on Highway 99, via West Ripon and Austin roads. (209) 953-8800.

Caswell Memorial State Park

Approximately 258 acres of valley oak woodland rimming the Stanislaus River are preserved here, providing visitors a chance to explore one of the San Joaquin Valley's last remnants of its once-extensive hardwood forests. Dense shrubs, 60-foot oaks, wild berries, animals, and numerous birds abound in this lush environment. The Oak Forest Nature Trail—about one mile in length—meanders along the river and through the woodlands. In

summer, fishing and swimming are popular activities along the river's banks and beaches; spring and fall are times of extraordinary tranquility in the riverside forest. An undeveloped corner of the park is a protected nesting area for great blue herons. A wooded picnic area gives a cool respite from summer heat, and more than 65 family campsites offer secluded camping with nearby restrooms and hot showers. Lifeguard service is not available, and during the summer when the water level is low, swimming may be unsafe. Check with the park staff for information about current conditions. Caswell Memorial State Park is five miles off Highway 99 via Austin Rd. exit south of Manteca. (209) 599-3810.

McConnell State Recreation Area

A canopy of towering trees at McConnell State Recreation Area beckons hot summer travelers to cool off and relax at the Merced River. There are over 70 acres of picnic, camping, and play areas, as well as fine swimming and fishing in the river. A group campsite is available, and there is a large group picnic area with fireplaces and a sizeable barbecue pit. Lifeguard service is not available. From the town of Delhi on

Highway 99 (just south of Turlock), follow the signs five miles southeast to McConnell. (209) 394-7755.

George J. Hatfield State Recreation Area

The Merced River surrounds this San Joaquin Valley oasis on three sides, offering swimming and fishing near the confluence of the Merced and San Joaquin Rivers. The well-kept lawns and oak woodlands, on land once inhabited by California Indians, contain shady picnic areas, 21 family campsites, and a group camping area. RVs are welcome, but there are no hookups. The 46-acre site is dotted with gracious, mature trees and abounds with wildlife, particularly birds. Lifeguard service is not available. From Interstate 5 take the Newman exit into Newman, and continue east on County Road J-18 for five miles; the park entrance is just past the San Joaquin River bridge. (209) 632-1852.

Fremont Ford State Recreation Area

At the bridge on Highway 140 between Merced and Gustine, anglers have day-use access to the San Joaquin River. The recreation area is completely undeveloped. (209) 826-1196.

California's Oak Trees

L ike islands in a sea of grass, great oaks have long stood watch over California's hills and valleys. Trees still live that once flickered in the glow of Indian camps, trees whose branches offered shade to Spanish explorers, Mexican cattle, and American settlers. A history of drought, flood, wind, and fire is written in their massive gnarled forms.

Rooted deeply in the past, every oak is also very much a part of the living present. For the deer, birds, and, rodents depending on its crop of acorns, an oak tree is the starting point of a food web that extends far across the countryside. To a host of smaller creatures, though, an oak tree is a self-contained universe, providing all needs and defining the limits of existence.

Despite their appeal to the eye and to the imagination, in many areas these ancient trees are disappearing—cleared for agriculture or land development, cut for fuel and fenceposts, or simply dying of old age. A basic element of the landscape—one that is purely, uniquely Californian—is gradually passing from the scene.

—John Werminski,
State Park Naturalist

Eight species of oak are native to California, including two that are endemic to the state's offshore islands. Valley oak, once prevalent alongside the rivers of the Central Valley, is the largest oak species in America, growing over 100 feet tall and living 500 to 600 years. Producing the biggest acorns of any variety, it provided many California Indian tribes with their single most important source of food. Since valley oaks thrive in rich, deep soil, early pioneers who settled near those trees were usually assured of fertile, productive farmland. Magnificent stands of valley oak may be enjoyed in riverside parks such as McConnell, George J. Hatfield, and Caswell Memorial.

In the foothills and low ranges, many oak species are found growing together or in close proximity. Valley oak, blue oak, leather oak, coast live oak, and interior live oak are well represented in Coast Range parks such as Annadel, Henry W. Coe, Fremont Peak, and Mount Diablo. Indian Grinding Rock State Historic Park in the Sierra foothills contains a large, flat limestone outcropping, pitted with over 1,000 mortars that were used by Miwok Indians to pound acorns into flour.

The California State Park System is using innovative land management and seed propagation techniques to protect and perpetuate oak forests on public lands. At Annadel State Park in Sonoma County, for example, a 500-acre tract of blue oak and Oregon oak is being rescued. Here, fire suppression policies have allowed Douglas-fir to spread quickly, forcing out young oaks that cannot compete well with the faster-growing conifers. At Angel Island State Park in Marin County,

plans call for several large stands of imported eucalyptus trees to be replaced with native oaks. In parks such as George J. Hatfield and Fort Tejon, valley oak is experiencing poor regeneration due in part to the mowing of park grounds and acorn foraging by deer. To help the trees get started, acorns are collected on site and germinated in pots. Once they have grown large enough, these trees will be transplanted back to their native environment. By using only local acorns, these oak tree nurseries help protect the genetic integrity of the park habitat. In the near future, each valley park will be raising a number of trees in this manner. Through conservation programs such as these, California's oak trees may yet remain with us as a valuable, and irreplaceable, resource.

(Opposite): Oaks shrouded in fog, Mount Diablo State Park. (Above): Blue oak at Millerton Lake State Recreation Area.

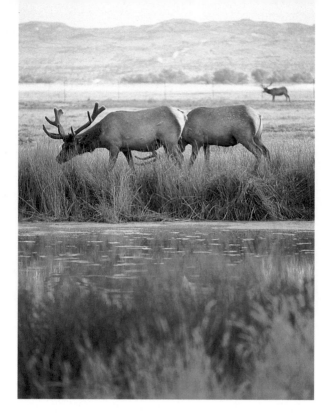

(Top): Tule elk bulls, Tule Elk State Reserve. (Above): Colonel Allensworth State Historic Park. (Opposite): San Luis Reservoir State Recreation Area.

San Luis Island

This 2,700-acre area was acquired in 1980-1981 in order to preserve a portion of the San Joaquin Valley in relatively undisturbed, natural condition for the benefit of present and future generations. The area protects native grassland in what is now the largest remaining unplowed area within California's great valley. Several rare and endangered species of native plants and animals are present. Vernal pools are abundant in the spring along with extensive stands of valley sacatan, a native bunch grass. The area is located about halfway between Turlock and Los Banos on the west side of State Highway 165 and includes frontage on both the San Joaquin River and Salt Slough. The area is undeveloped at this time and there is no safe access or parking available. (209) 826-1196.

San Luis Reservoir State Recreation Area

Three artifical lakes within San Luis Reservoir State Recreation Area—San Luis Reservoir, O'Neill Forebay, and Los Banos Creek Reservoir—have become major recreational resources. Fishing, by boat or from shore, is no doubt the foremost activity at the lakes. The plentiful fish population includes

Joaquin Valley dedicated to improving the economic and social status of black people. Colonel Allen Allensworth, a former slave, Union soldier, and the highest ranking black officer and army chaplain of his time, led the group as they built and sustained a successful and active community. The colonel's death, a severe drop in the region's water table, and changes in the valley's routes of commerce all played a role in the eventual demise of the town of Allensworth. Today, restored buildings and a visitor center, which includes a 30-minute film, are open to the public. A yearly rededication ceremony reaffirms the vision of these pioneers. Colonel Allensworth State Historic Park includes a shaded picnic area and a 15-site campground. Programs and guided tours for groups may be arranged in advance. Museum hours are 10 to 4. From Highway 99 in Earlimart, the park is seven miles west via County Rd. J-22 and Highway 43. (805) 849-3433.

Tule Elk State Reserve
When central California was being cleared and settled in the 1800s, vast herds of tule elk were reduced to near-extinction by hunting and loss of habitat. It was thought that only two tule elk remained in 1874 when cattle-man Henry Miller began his 50-year effort to save them. Given protection on his baronial ranch, the tule elk came back from the brink of extinction; 28 of the animals were counted in an 1895 census, and their numbers grew steadily thereafter. In 1932, the small herd was given permanent protection in a 953-acre property, site of today's Tule Elk State Reserve. Individuals from this herd in the southern San Joaquin Valley were successfully transplanted to the Owens Valley in Inyo County, the Cache Creek area of Colusa County, and other areas where free-roaming herds of tule elk can be found today. Visitors can use the reserve's well-shaded picnic area and observe the elk grazing in the fields. Tule elk are most active from late summer through early autumn; a pair of binoculars is advisable for better viewing. The reserve is south of Buttonwillow and just a few minutes drive west of Interstate 5 via the Stockdale Highway. (209) 822-2332.

black and striped bass, bluegill, catfish, and crappie. Waterskiing, windsurfing, swimming, bird watching, and picnicking draw weekend crowds; designated areas are set aside where hunters are welcome to seek fowl, deer, rabbits, and wild pigs in season. At O'Neill Forebay, a section of the California Aqueduct Bikeway begins its 70-mile journey toward Bethany Reservoir.

Camping sites are found at each lake: at San Luis Reservoir, the Basalt Area has nearly 80 improved sites with hot showers and space for trailers and campers up to 37 feet long (no hookups); at Los Banos Creek Reservoir there are 20 primitive sites and an equestrian camp; at O'Neill Forebay, unreserved primitive space can accommodate up to 500 RVs. From Interstate 5 near Los Banos, Highway 152 leads west a few miles to O'Neill Forebay and San Luis Reservoir. Smaller and calmer, the Los Banos Creek Reservoir is several miles south, just west of Interstate 5. Access to the area is by way of Highway 152 east of Interstate 5. Follow the signs south on county roads. (209) 826-1196.

Colonel Allensworth State Historic Park
In 1908, a handful of black Americans established a town in the southern San

CHAPTER FIVE

Southern California Coast

The warm and sandy shoreline that we call the Southern California coast begins just south of Point Conception where the shore swings east and then gradually curves southward to the Mexican border. Here ocean currents eddy, bringing mild ocean water temperatures that invite swimming much of the year. These warm-water shores, including 40 state beaches and parks, are Southern California's most popular recreational amenity. Along with the beaches themselves, however, there are also some fascinating state historic parks and mountainous upland areas with deep canyons and many miles of hiking trail.

Stretching east from Point Conception, the Santa Ynez Mountains form a ridge above the ocean where three pleasant, seaside camping parks are found just west of Santa Barbara: Gaviota, Refugio, and El Capitan. Visitors to this area may camp at nearby Carpinteria State Beach or visit downtown Santa Barbara's El Presidio de Santa Barbara State Historic Park, which preserves a 200-year-old Spanish-California fortification. A little farther south, state beaches near the city of Ventura include Emma Wood, San Buenaventura, and McGrath State Beach, which is located at the mouth of the Santa Clara River, a popular spot for bird watching.

Three state parks in the Santa Monica Mountains—Point Mugu, Malibu Creek, and Topanga—have extensive trail systems that invite exploration of this rugged range that lies close beside the nation's second-largest city. A string of state beaches line the scenic 35-mile shore along the southern flank of this transverse range, which rises dramatically above the Pacific. State beaches, from Leo Carrillo to Topanga, offer a wide spectrum of seaside recreation, including swimming, surfing, camping, picnicking, hiking, surf fishing, wind surfing, diving, and lots of tide pools, coves, and caves. Scattered across the Los Angeles metropolitan area and nearby valleys is a diverse collection of parks, including adobes from the Spanish and Mexican eras at Los Encinos and Pio Pico state parks, a Civil War army post in Wilmington, and two very different but equally interesting examples of 20th-century art and architecture—Pan Pacific Auditorium and Watts Towers.

Near Santa Monica, the coast turns southward in a 20-mile-long sweep of wide, sandy shoreline where state beaches such as Dockweiler, Manhattan, and Redondo are popular throughout most of the year. The Orange County coastline also features some very popular state beaches, such as Bolsa Chica (with its adjacent wetlands) and Huntington State Beach. Crystal Cove State Park, with both beach front and coastal foothill acreage, preserves nearly 2,800 acres of open space in this increasingly urban region.

Northern San Diego County has a number of excellent state beaches, many of which are located at the foot of sandstone cliffs, with facilities on the blufftops above. Visitors to this area will find campgrounds at San Onofre, South Carlsbad, and San Elijo state beaches.

In addition to state beaches that offer some of the warmest water and best swimming and surfing in California, the San Diego area can also boast of three unique natural or historic areas that are protected by state park status: Torrey Pines State Reserve holds one of the only two stands of Torrey pine in the world; San Pasqual Battlefield State Historic Park contains the 1846 battlefield where a violent skirmish took place during the Mexican-American War; Old Town San Diego State Historic Park preserves and recreates one of California's first Spanish settlements.

(Opposite): Sunset on Huntington Beach. (Above): Colorful echevaria at Malibu Creek.

(Top): California Poppies, (Middle): Harbor Seals at Carpinteria Beach, (Above): Delicate wild viscaria.

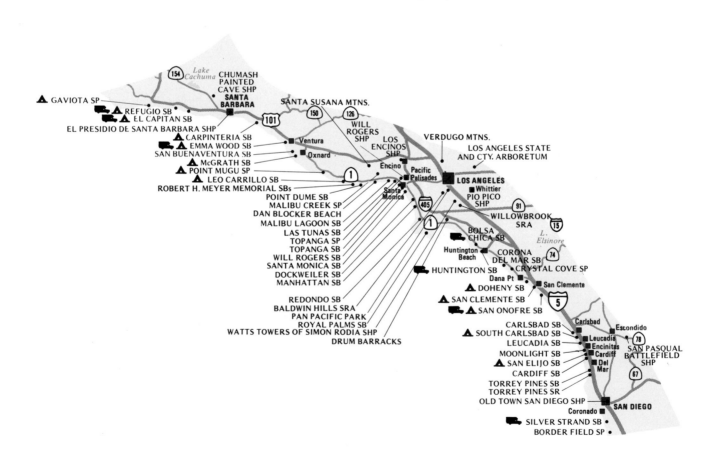

Santa Barbara Area

Gaviota State Park

This section of coast was first called *gaviota* (seagull) by soldiers of the Portola Expedition in 1769. The sandy cove at the mouth of Gaviota Creek is a popular spot for swimming, picnicking, and surf fishing. A pier on the west end of the beach has a three-ton boat launch, frequently used by divers and surfers headed toward the waters near Point Conception. Fifty-four campsites are nestled among tamarisk trees along Gaviota Creek; 36 of the sites can accommodate RVs to 30 feet. A Southern Pacific railroad trestle crosses the creek above the day-use parking lot. Groceries, fishing tackle, and bait are available at a small store in the park.

Visitors can explore the upland portions of this park from a trailhead parking area on the frontage road just south of where Highway 1 separates from U.S. Highway 101, about 2½ miles north of the main park entrance. A short walk from the parking area will get you to a warm sulphur spring. From there, a steep fire road continues up to 2,458-foot Gaviota Peak, from which there is a spectacular view of the coast and Channel Islands. The entrance to Gaviota State Park is on U.S. Highway 101, 33 miles west of Santa Barbara. (805) 968-1033.

Refugio State Beach

Palm trees line the shore near the mouth of Refugio Creek and lend a tropical feeling to this picturesque beach. The park's 1½ miles of shoreline includes swimming and surfing areas, grassy picnic grounds, and 85 developed campsites (vehicles up to 30 feet), as well as a store, hot showers, and laundry tubs. A blufftop bikeway connects with El Capitan State Beach, 2½ miles to the east. The entrance is on Refugio Rd., a marked exit off U.S. Highway 101, 23 miles northwest of Santa Barbara. (805) 968-1033.

El Capitan State Beach

Stands of sycamore and oak along the banks of El Capitan Creek and nearby bluffs give this park a charming, woodsy atmosphere. Tide pools are found along the rocky shoreline where the creek meets the sea. A sandy beach with swimming and surfing areas below the blufftops is reached by stairs or pathways. The park has a 140-site developed campground that can accommodate RVs up to 30 feet, an RV dump station, picnic areas, and a nature trail. A hike-bike camp is located at the edge of the bikeway that connects with nearby Refugio State Beach. Entrance is from U.S. Highway 101, 17 miles west of Santa Barbara. (805) 968-1033.

(Top): El Capitan State Beach. (Above): Painted Cave State Historic Park.

Chumash Painted Cave State Historic Park

This small park in a steep canyon above Santa Barbara preserves a fine example of Native American art. Symbols painted by Chumash Indians cover the side walls of a small sandstone rockshelter, which is protected from vandals by a metal grate over its entrance. Go eight miles west on Highway 154 from U.S. Highway 101, turn right onto Painted Cave Rd., and proceed two miles to the park. Parking and turnaround space is limited. Large camper vans and vehicles pulling trailers should avoid this road if possible, or return to Highway 154 by continuing uphill past the community of Painted Cave, and turn west on East Camino Cielo. (805) 968-3294.

Carpinteria State Beach.

El Presidio de Santa Barbara State Historic Park
During the 18th century, Spain established four presidios in California. Today, only one building and parts of another remain of the outpost in Santa Barbara, which was a military and governmental headquarters for the territory between Los Angeles and San Luis Obispo from 1782 until the American era in 1846. Built around a square, 400 feet to a side, many of the old adobe buildings and walls have vanished, but are being rebuilt through the efforts of the Santa Barbara Trust for Historic Preservation, operator of the park, and the California Conservation Corps. Two original structures have been restored, including El Cuartel, Santa Barbara's oldest adobe. Handmade adobe blocks have been used to reconstruct the Padres' Quarters and Presidio Chapel. El Presidio is located in downtown Santa Barbara on Cañon Perdido between Anacapa and Santa Barbara streets. (805) 966-9719.

Carpinteria State Beach
Carpinteria State Beach offers nearly a mile of gently sloping beach, ideal for swimming and surf fishing. At low tide, tide pools can be explored on nearby Carpinteria Reef. Chumash Indians established a settlement here, close to the tar pits that supplied them with waterproof caulking material for

their seagoing canoes. Their boat works led the Spaniards to name it La Carpinteria, or "carpentry shop." Facilities include a large campground, day-use parking, and picnic pavilions. The 262 developed campsites include 86 with hookups; RVs up to 30 feet can be accommodated. Access is via Highway 224, a marked exit on U.S. Highway 101. (805) 684-2811 or 654-4611.

Ventura Area

Emma Wood State Beach
The main entrance to this state beach is one mile northwest of Ventura at the intersection of Main St. and U.S. Highway 101, near the mouth of the Ventura River. This part of the park features a grassy area for groups and a campground for hikers and bikers. A cobble beach with good views of Anacapa Island is nearby, and dolphins are often visible from the beach. Visitors enjoy surfing, swimming, and surf fishing. At the northern end of the park, family campsites are operated by the County of Ventura. There are 61 campsites spread over a mile-long section of the old Pacific Coast Highway, which runs parallel to the Southern Pacific Railroad right of way (805) 643-7532 or 654-4611. County of Ventura section: (805) 654-3951.

San Buenaventura State Beach
This broad, sandy beach, protected from erosion by a series of small rock jetties, is a popular destination for swimming, surfing, or fishing. Behind the beach is a grassy picnic area dotted with pines and Monterey cypress. A 1,700-foot pier has a snack bar, restaurant, and bait shop. The bike path that runs the length of the park connects with Ventura to the south and Emma Wood State Beach to the northwest. The park entrance is off Harbor Blvd., just north of the Seaward Ave. exit from U.S. Highway 101. (805) 654-4611.

McGrath State Beach
McGrath State Beach near the mouth of the Santa Clara River is a favorite with bird watchers and nature lovers. Its 174 developed campsites are sheltered among stands of wind-sculpted trees. A nature trail through dense

Statue of St. Francis of Assisi in the Santa Barbara Presidio Chapel.

thickets of willow leads to the Santa Clara Estuary Natural Preserve, home to three species of endangered birds and a haven for a variety of small wildlife. At the park's southern end is a fresh-water lake where over 200 bird species have been sighted. Two miles of dune-fringed beach invite surfing and fishing; due to strong currents and riptides, use caution when swimming. The entrance is off Harbor Blvd. in Oxnard, just south of the Santa Clara River. (805) 654-4744 or 654-4611.

Santa Monica Mountains

Point Mugu State Park

The Santa Monica Mountains are part of the Transverse Range, the only east-west trending mountain range in coastal California. The Santa Monicas stretch 46 miles, from the Los Angeles River in the heart of the city west to Point Mugu. They reach a scenic climax in the mighty rock ramparts of the 6,000-acre Boney Mountain State Wilderness Area within Point Mugu State Park. The 13,360-acre park also includes La Jolla Valley, a secluded preserve of rare, native tall grasses, and Big Sycamore Canyon, which drops some 500 feet in seven miles, and creates a broad savanna, edged with majestic syca-mores and live oaks. Visitors can hike in shady canyons, rolling meadows, slopes of dense chaparral and coastal sage scrub, or seaside stands of giant coreopsis.

The park is home to a variety of wildlife, including deer, foxes, mountain lions, bobcats, falcons, owls, hawks, and eagles. Prevailing winds have blown an impressive sand dune halfway up the mountain opposite La Jolla Beach. Three miles of rocky shore and cliffs shelter two sandy beaches: Sycamore Cove, with a picnic area, and La Jolla Beach, with 85 primitive campsites. Big Sycamore Canyon has 55 developed campsites (RVs to 31 feet). There is a hike-in camp in La Jolla Valley. More than 50 miles of trail invite exploration on foot, by bike (fire roads only), or horseback. The south entrance is on Pacific Coast Highway, 31 miles west of Santa Monica. A north entrance on Potrero Rd. south of Newbury Park provides trail access to upper Big Sycamore Canyon. (818) 706-1310 or (805) 488-5223.

(Top): San Buenaventura Beach State Park. (Above): Annual Century Bike Race, Emma Wood State Beach.

Leo Carrillo State Beach

Named in honor of a famous radio and television actor who served on the Park and Recreation Commission during the 1950s, Leo Carrillo State Beach offers visitors a wide spectrum of choices for coastal recreation. Good swimming, wind surfing, and surf fishing are enjoyed along its 1½ miles of ocean frontage. Sequit Point offers some of the area's best surfing and diving, and the park's tide pools, coastal caves, and offshore reefs invite exploration. Two sycamore-shaded campgrounds are located in the 2,000-acre park: Canyon Campground has 138 family campsites and can accommodate 31-foot motor homes; the group campground can accommodate up to 50 people. North Beach Campground has 32 family campsites for self-contained vehicles that are less than eight feet high. Hike-and-bike campsites are also found in the park. Hikers can enter Arroyo Sequit Canyon or ascend slopes to scenic overlooks, 1,000 feet above the Pacific Ocean. The Nicholas Flat Trail, popular with energetic hikers, climbs up to a pond at Nicholas Flat, passing various plant communities of the Santa Monica Mountains along the way. Interpretive activities are offered throughout the year, including nature walks and campfire programs. A small visitor center with interpretive displays is located adjacent to the North Beach

parking lot. Leo Carrillo State Beach is 25 miles west of Santa Monica on Pacific Coast Highway. (805) 987-3303 or (818) 706-1310

Malibu Creek State Park

This delightful 6,600-acre park gives some visitors a sense of deja vu because the area was used for many years by Twentieth Century Fox as a location for film and television productions. More importantly, it protects some of the most interesting natural features of Malibu Creek — the principal watercourse of the Santa Monica Mountains. From high on Boney Mountain to its mouth at Malibu Lagoon, the 25-mile creek drains 100 square miles and creates the only major water gap in the range. Malibu Creek State Park preserves four oxbow bends in rugged Triunfo Canyon and the dramatic gorge of Malibu Canyon. A center of Chumash life for centuries, homesteaded in the 19th century, and a movie ranch in the 1940s, the land became a California state park in 1976. Today it offers the refreshment of a rugged mountain environment, just 25 miles from downtown Los Angeles. Visitors enjoy picnicking, hiking, and riding bicycles or horses on the fire roads. Fifteen miles of streamside trail pass through oak and sycamore woodlands and across chaparral-covered slopes. A developed campground with 60 sites

is suitable for single-car family, tent camping. The park entrance is on Las Virgenes Rd. (Route N1), four miles south of U.S. Highway 101. (818) 706-8809 or 706-1310.

Topanga State Park

Topanga State Park preserves 9,181 acres of chaparral-covered ridge and canyon country in the rugged Santa Monica Mountains. Located entirely within the Los Angeles city limits, this park is considered the world's largest wildland within the boundaries of a major city. The park's 32 miles of trails traverse ridge tops, dip into Santa Ynez, Los Liones, Temescal, and Rustic Canyons, and lead to a hike-in camp beside a spring. Trails also climb to the top of 2,126-foot Temescal Peak, which offers superb views east toward distant mountain ranges and west over the Channel Islands. Although prohibited on hiking trails, bicyclists can ride on an extensive system of fire roads. Within the park are five distinct plant communities — chaparral, coastal sage scrub, oak woodland, grass woodland, and riparian woodland; upper Santa Ynez Canyon is well-known for its spring wildflower displays. The park's main entrance is on Entrada Rd., east of Topanga Canyon Blvd. (Highway 27), at a point eight miles south of U.S. Highway 101. (213) 455-2465 or (818) 706-1310.

Malibu Area

Robert H. Meyer Memorial State Beach

A number of cove or cliff-foot strands known as "pocket beaches" lie midway between Leo Carrillo and Point Dume State Beaches. Parcels of nine to 18 acres, they have parking for 16 to 20 cars at blufftop and paths down to the beach. Signs on Pacific Coast Highway call them out by name: El Pescador, La Piedra, El Matador. (818) 706-1310.

(Top): Topanga State Park. (Above): Scuba divers at Leo Carrillo State Beach.

Paradise Cove, Point Dume State Beach.

Point Dume State Beach

Point Dume State Beach features headlands, cliffs, secluded coves, and tide pools, as well as Westward Beach, a large sandy stretch of shore that is managed by Los Angeles County. Popular activities include swimming, surfing, scuba diving, and fishing. The 215-foot-high Point Dume Headland offers a fine view of the coast and is a good place to watch migrating California gray whales between November and May. This is also one of the few places on the West Coast where the sun (and moon) can be seen rising over the Pacific. The 34-acre park contains a stand of the rare giant coreopsis, which has showy yellow flowers in winter. There is a parking area and restrooms. Enter from Westward Rd., 18 miles west of Santa Monica. (213) 305-9503 or (818) 706-1310.

Dan Blocker Beach

Still listed on some maps as Corral State Beach, this mile-long stretch of sand is located right where the Pacific Coast Highway dips down to shore level between the mouths of Corral and Solstice canyons. Visitors enjoy swimming, scuba diving, picnicking, or surf fishing. Access is at Pacific Coast Highway and Corral Canyon Rd., 13 miles west of Santa Monica. (213) 620-3342.

Malibu Lagoon State Beach

Part of this park, including the famous Surfrider Beach, is operated by Los Angeles County. The other part, run by the state, includes the Adamson House and garden, the lagoon where Malibu Creek meets the sea, a fishing and party-boat pier often seen on film, and the Malibu Bluffs across Pacific Coast Highway from Pepperdine University. Built in 1929, the interior of the beautifully crafted Adamson House (a National Historic Landmark) is decorated with colorful Malibu tile that was made nearby as a family enterprise during the 1920s. Its seven-car garage has been converted to a museum (open Wednesday through Saturday, 10 to 2) that houses a variety of exhibits about Malibu's history, from Chumash fishing ground to movie colony. The lagoon area is laced with paths and bridges, affording birders a chance to see some of the 200 species found in this rare remnant of coastal wetland.

Facilities include restrooms and a picnic area. Entrances and parking are at both ends of the Malibu Creek bridge, 10 miles west of Santa Monica. (213) 456-8432 or (818) 706-1310. For beach information: (213) 456-9497.

Las Tunas State Beach

Las Tunas State Beach derives its name from the area's once-extensive stands of prickly pear cactus—called *tunas* in Spanish. The small, sandy beach is popular with scuba divers, most of whom enjoy a nearby offshore reef. A variety of surf fish attracts anglers. Parking is on the road shoulder. This state beach, operated by Los Angeles County, is located on Pacific Coast Highway, one mile west of Topanga Canyon Blvd. (213) 305-9503.

Topanga State Beach

This mile-long, narrow beach at the mouth of Topanga Canyon is is a favorite of surfers and swimmers. Restrooms and parking space are provided. Access is from Pacific Coast Highway at Topanga Canyon Blvd. in Malibu. It is operated by Los Angeles County. (213) 455-2465.

California's Rare and Wonderful Plant World

California has an astonishing diversity of native plants, with over 5,000 species occurring within the state boundaries. Nearly one third of them are endemic, plants that are native to California and nowhere else—a higher proportion than in any other state in the Union. Many plant species have never been common, and are now increasingly endangered by the state's swelling human population and the accompanying conversion of natural landscapes to residential, industrial, or agricultural use. Not only are wilderness values thus threatened, but genetic possibliites of incalculable value in the fields of medicine, agriculture, and industry are lost forever. Native vegetation also plays an important role in watershed management.

Over 1,000 of California's native plant species are sufficiently rare to be listed and monitored by various agencies, and many of them are protected within state parks, including coast redwoods, giant sequoias, Joshua trees, and native fan palms. State parks also preserve unique plant communities, such as unusual chaparral associations in the Santa Monica Mountains, coniferous forests on Mount San Jacinto and in the Cuyamaca Mountains, and the ocotillo-cactus scrub in the Anza-Borrego Desert.

State reserves are established primarily to give protection to certain plant or animal species and help ensure their survival. For example, reserves protect the rare Torrey pine north of San Diego, the Monterey and Gowen cypresses at Point Lobos, the California poppy in the Antelope Valley, and azaleas and rhododendrons on the North Coast. State reserves may also contain unusual plant communities, such as the pygmy forest areas of Jug Handle State Reserve.

Natural preserves are tracts set aside within larger park units. They usually protect sensitive plant assemblages; examples include a forest of coast redwood, sitka spruce, and grand fir in Harry A. Merlo State Recreation Area, sand dune plant communities in Pismo Dunes State Vehicular Recreation Area, native grasses in Point Mugu State Park, Mojave Desert plants in Red Rock Canyon State Park, and wetland habitats for birds in a number of coastal parks.

A surprising number of parks contain rare and endangered species or unusual plant communities that are not well publicized although their whereabouts are known to park personnel and botanists. Such sites may benefit from the extra habitat protection that a lack of publicity sometimes provides.

i): Rhododendrons and redwood trees, Del Norte woods State Park. (Above): Spring wildflowers many plant enthusiasts.

San Fernando Valley Area

Los Encinos State Historic Park

For many centuries, a fresh, warm water spring attracted human beings to this site—a natural stopping point along the age-old travel route between Sepulveda Pass and Topanga Pass. In 1769, a Spanish exploratory expedition under Captain Gaspar de Portola stopped here beside an Indian village. The property's first rancher built an adobe house on this land in 1849. Stagecoaches made regular stopovers here after 1858, and in 1872 Basque sheepherders constructed a stone house, reminiscent of dwellings in their homeland. This five-acre park preserves several of these historic structures and tours of the adobe ranch house and outbuildings are conducted on a regular basis. Visitors enjoy picnics near the spring, which is now contained in a guitar-shaped pond. Los Encinos State Historic Park is located at 16756 Moorpark St. in Encino. (818) 784-4849.

Santa Susana Mountains

Still in the acquisition stage, this 428-acre park includes sections of an 1890s wagon road and the later Santa Susana Pass Rd., forerunners of today's Simi Valley (118) Freeway. The history of the Santa Susana Mountains area is recalled here by the presence of Indian mortar holes and remnants of a stagecoach road that dates from 1860. The best access to trails is from Chatsworth Park at the end of Devonshire St., west from Highway 27. (213) 620-3342.

Verdugo Mountains

The Verdugos are a free-standing mini-range—an island that rises above the adjacent urbanized flatlands and foot-hills. Trails go through chaparral, across shady, oak-forested slopes, and along sycamore-lined streams. Hikers who climb to the park's 3,126-foot-high point are rewarded with fine views of the surrounding mountains, the San Gabriel and San Fernando valleys, and the Los Angeles plain. A fire road (closed to private vehicles) connects with roads in adjacent parks and open space land. Still in the acquisition stage, this 200-acre park can be entered from La Tuna Canyon Rd., just west of the 210 Freeway. (213) 620-3342.

Santa Monica Bay

Will Rogers State Beach

This is the northernmost of Santa Monica Bay's heavily used swimming and surfing beaches. Popular activities at Will Rogers State Beach are swimming, surfing, body surfing, and skin diving. Facilities include volleyball courts, playground and gymnastic equipment, as well as a bike path and walkway. The bike path—the South Bay Bicycle Trail—is the most heavily used in Southern California. It begins here and runs 19.1 miles along the shore through Santa Monica State Beach to Redondo State Beach in Torrance. The state beach extends along 1¾ miles of shore; parking lots are located off Pacific Coast Highway, near the intersection with Temescal Canyon Rd. The beach is operated by Los Angeles County. (213) 305-9545 or 394-3266.

Santa Monica State Beach

One of the broadest sandy beaches in Southern California, Santa Monica State Beach has over three miles of ocean front with swimming and surfing areas, playgrounds, volleyball courts, and gymnastic equipment. Beach visitors stroll on the Santa Monica Municipal Pier and spin on its famous carousel. Santa Monica State Beach is operated by the City of Santa Monica and is served by a series of parking lots along Pacific Coast Highway. (213) 305-9545 or 394-3266.

Dockweiler State Beach

This wide beach (beneath the takeoff path from Los Angeles International Airport) is one of the few at which fires are permitted; fire rings are provided. Dockweiler's 3⅓ miles of shoreline includes swimming and surfing areas. Facilities feature storage for small sail-boats, a bikeway, picnic areas, and an RV campground. Dockweiler State Beach is operated by Los Angeles County and is located at the western terminus of Imperial Highway in Playa del Rey. The park entrance is on Vista del Mar. (213) 305-9503.

Manhattan State Beach

These two miles of broad, sandy beach are popular for swimming, surfing, and fishing. Facilities include over 100

(Top): Watts Towers, Watts Towers of Simon Rodia State Historic Park. (Above): Polo players at Will Rogers State Historic Park. (Opposite): Volleyball enthusiasts, Manhattan State Beach.

volleyball courts, restrooms, and limited parking areas. The Strand, a concrete promenade, is used for walking, jogging, and skating; there is also a bike path. The Manhattan Beach Pier features a number of exhibits about marine life. Manhattan State Beach is operated by Los Angeles County and is located immediately west of the Strand in Manhattan Beach. (213) 372-2166.

Redondo State Beach
Sandy and wide, this 1½-mile stretch of beach beneath low bluffs is just north of Palos Verdes Peninsula. Visitors enjoy swimming, surfing, and fishing. Restrooms and volleyball courts are provided. The South Bay Bicycle Trail runs the length of the beach, as does a paved footpath. Redondo State Beach is operated by Los Angeles County and is located west of Esplanade in Redondo Beach. (213) 305-9545.

Los Angeles Metropolitan Area

Will Rogers State Historic Park
The famous humorist, writer, and actor lived in this house, kept horses, and generally got away from it all here during the 1920s and '30s. Today the house, its furnishings, and its 186 acres of open space recall the good life during the 1920s—a time when one could buy a place just outside the city big enough

for a golf course, stables, riding and roping rings, and polo field. (It had no pool, so Rogers bought land next to the beach that bears his name today.) Visitors can tour the house and grounds, picnic, or watch a weekend polo match. Trails lead into adjacent Topanga State Park, making this a good starting point for a hike. Will Rogers State Historic Park is located at 14235 Sunset Blvd. in Pacific Palisades. (213) 372-2166.

Pan Pacific Park
This urban park has picnic and play areas, sport fields, and an outdoor amphitheater. Until fire destroyed it in May 1989, it also preserved the Pan Pacific Auditorium—an acclaimed classic of Depression-era architecture. The auditorium featured a Streamline Moderne façade and four flashy towers. The barn-like hall, famed for auto shows, sports events, and spectacles, was due to be remodeled. Pan Pacific Park is operated by Los Angeles County and is located at 7600 Beverly Blvd. in Los Angeles. (818) 798-1173.

Watts Towers of Simon Rodia State Historic Park
In the 1950s and 1960s these hand-sculpted towers were one of the most widely publicized of Los Angeles landmarks. There are nine structures, ranging in height from 13 to over 100 feet.

Hailed as a triumph of folk art, the Watts Towers were constructed from steel pipes and rods, wrapped with wire mesh, coated with mortar, and embedded with 70,000 pieces of porcelain, tile, and glass. Italian immigrant Simon Rodia, who built them over a period of 33 years without the aid of scaffolds, welding torch, or other power equipment, walked away from his creation in 1954 when he had finished. Today, the state historic park is operated by the City of Los Angeles and is undergoing long-term restoration. Call for a schedule of tours of the grounds. The Watts Towers are at located at 1765 East 107th St., in Los Angeles. (213) 933-1094 or (818) 798-1173.

Kenneth Hahn State Recreation Area
Set among rolling, grassy hills with a view of Los Angeles to the north, Kenneth Hahn (formerly Baldwin Hills) State Recreation Area has picnic and play areas, two fishing lakes, a man-made stream, hiking trails, and an Olympic Forest—planted with one tree for each of the 140 nations that participated in the 1984 games in Los Angeles. It also contains the site of the 1932 Olympic Village for athletes in the Tenth Olympiad. The park is operated by Los Angeles County; its entrance is at 4100 South La Cienega Blvd. in Baldwin Hills. (213) 291-0199.

Pio Pico State Historic Park

This three-acre park was the center of an 8,891-acre Mexican-era ranch and preserves the adobe residence of Pio Pico, the last governor of Mexican California. Pio Pico's parents came to California in 1775 with the Anza expedition. He worked his way to wealth and power—became the owner of half a million acres of prime Southern California land. During the American era he built a 20-room mansion on this site and rebuilt it after the great flood of 1884. He also built Pico House on the Los Angeles Plaza, the Southwest's most elegant hotel during its heyday in the 1870s. In later life, his fortune gradually dwindled until at the age of 90 he lost everything and was even evicted from the mansion. He died in 1894 in absolute poverty. The mansion was severely damaged by an earthquake in 1987 and was closed to the public pending the completion of major repairs. The grounds remain open for picnicking and day use Wednesday through Sunday. The park is located just west of the 605 Freeway, at the corner of Pioneer and Whittier blvds. in Whittier. (213) 695-1217.

Drum Barracks Civil War Museum

As an outgrowth of the U.S. Army's policy to expand into the far West, a base was established in Wilmington in 1859. The new fort, known as Drum Barracks, became the Army supply depot for Southern California, Arizona, and New Mexico. In 1862, units of the California Column set out from here, combining forces in the desert to turn back a Confederate incursion near Tucson. Only the 16-room junior officers' quarters, built of materials brought around the Horn, remain from the dozen original structures that served 400 soldiers until the post closed in 1866. Museum displays feature period furniture, portraits, models, a dispensary, and such artifacts as an operable Gatling gun. Drum Barracks Civil War Museum is operated by the City of Los Angeles and is located at 1053 Cary Ave. in Wilmington. (213) 548-7509.

Royal Palms State Beach

Royal Palms State Beach, operated by Los Angeles County, combines rocky shoreline and sandy coves near White's

Sandstone Bluffs canyon, San Onofre State Beach.

Point on the Palos Verdes Peninsula. Beach visitors can explore tide pools, fish, or scuba dive. Ruins of the Royal Palms Hotel, built here in 1915, can still be seen, along with a stand of palms and overgrown landscaping. White's Point County Beach, with more rocky shore, adjoins to the southeast. Access is at the foot of Western Ave. in San Pedro. (213) 305-9503.

Orange County

Bolsa Chica State Beach

This broad, level expanse of sand extends three miles from Seal Beach to Huntington Beach City Pier. A bikeway connects it with Huntington State Beach, about seven miles south. Bolsa Chica State Beach has 50 campsites suitable for self-contained RVs, fire rings, showers and dressing rooms, a paved ramp for wheelchair access, concessions, and 2,500 parking spaces. The 1,000-acre Bolsa Chica Ecological Reserve, operated by the California Department of Fish and Game, is across the road from the beach and can be explored via a 1½-mile loop trail. One of Orange County's few remaining tracts of undeveloped coastal wetland, the reserve is an important bird habitat where over 200 shorebird and waterfowl species have been sighted. The state beach entrance is on Pacific Coast Highway about 1½ miles south of Warner Ave. (714) 846-3460 or 848-1566.

Huntington State Beach

This popular seaside playground extends two miles from Beach Blvd. in Huntington Beach south to the Santa Ana River on the Newport Beach boundary. Visitors enjoy swimming, sunbathing, surf fishing, bicycling, picnicking, beachcombing, and world-famous surfing. It has fire rings, showers and dressing rooms, a paved ramp for wheelchair access, a bikeway, a store, and 2,500 parking spaces. A five-acre natural preserve beside the river protects sensitive nesting areas of the California least tern. Across the highway from the state beach is the 114-acre Huntington Beach Wetlands, operated by the California Department of Fish and Game. The entrance to Huntington State Beach is opposite Magnolia Ave. on Pacific Coast Highway. (714) 536-1454 or 536-1455.

Corona Del Mar State Beach

Framed by dramatic cliffs and the rock jetty that forms the east entrance of Newport Harbor, this half-mile stretch of beach attracts swimmers, surfers, and divers. This beach is operated by the City of Newport Beach. The beach parking lot and day-use facilities can be reached via an access road near the intersection of Iris St. and Ocean Blvd in Corona del Mar. (714) 644-3044.

Crystal Cove State Park

Crystal Cove State Park is the last major open space on the Orange County coast. Its 2,791 acres include wooded Moro Canyon in the San Joaquin Hills and 3¼ miles of scenic shoreline. Visitors come to explore tide pools and sandy coves, and to fish, dive, or sunbathe. The offshore area to a depth of 120 feet is designated as an underwater park. Its submarine beauty and diversity make Crystal Cove State Park one of California's prime skin- and scuba-diving locations. The small coastal community of Crystal Cove has changed little since its establishment in the 1920s and has recently been added to the National Register of Historic Places. Park facilities include an environmental campground, showers, picnic areas, and 23 miles of trails for hiking, cycling and horseback riding. Crystal Cove State Park is between Corona Del Mar and Laguna Beach,

San Clemente State Beach.

just off Pacific Coast Highway (714) 494-3539 or 848-1566.

Doheny State Beach

This 62-acre park at the mouth of San Juan Creek has a mile of wide, sandy beach for swimming, surfing, and surf fishing. A rocky area at the beach's northern end attracts divers and anglers. The San Juan Creek Bike Trail begins just north of the beach. The creek beside Dana Point Marina divides facilities into two sections: the area west of the creek is reserved for day use; 162 developed campsites are located east of the creek. The park entrance is on Del Obispo St., just seaward of Pacific Coast Highway in Dana Point. (714) 496-6171 or 492-0802.

San Clemente State Beach

San Clemente State Beach has a landscaped blufftop with picnic areas and a developed campground with 157 sites (72 with hookups). Trails lead down to a mile-long beach that is popular for surfing, body surfing, swimming, and skin diving. To reach the park, take the

Avenida Calafia exit off Interstate 5 near the south end of San Clemente. (714) 492-3156 or 492-0802.

San Diego County

San Onofre State Beach

San Onofre State Beach contains chaparral-covered coastal terrace, sandstone cliffs, and 3½ miles of sandy shore that can be reached by trail from the blufftop. The park also includes a marshy area where San Mateo Creek meets the shoreline, and Trestles Beach, a well-known California surfing spot. Whales, dolphins, and sea lions often cavort offshore. Camping areas (221 developed sites) with restrooms and cold-water outdoor showers are found above the beach along a stretch of what used to be the coast highway. Twenty walk-in campsites sites are found at Echo Arch. Take the Basilone Rd. exit off Interstate 5 (near the San Diego and Orange county line) and proceed about three miles south to the park entrance. (714) 492-4872 or 492-0802.

Carlsbad State Beach

This mile-long beach at the foot of coastal bluffs has gentle surf and is a favorite of swimmers, surfers, anglers, and picnickers. Exit Interstate 5 at Tamarack Ave. and go southwest to Carlsbad Blvd. (Route S21). (619) 729-8947.

South Carlsbad State Beach

The large blufftop campground (226 developed sites) at South Carlsbad State Beach is very popular in summer, and advance reservations are therefore advised. Stairs lead to the beach, where swimming, fishing, skin diving, and surfing are enjoyed. Take Palomar Airport Rd. west from Interstate 5 to Carlsbad Blvd. (Route S21), then head south. (619) 438-3143 or 729-8947.

Leucadia State Beach

Swimming, surfing, fishing, and picnicking are among the popular pastimes enjoyed at this small, rocky beach in the City of Encinitas. Beach access is via an improved trail at the foot of Leucadia Blvd., west of Interstate 5. (619) 729-8947.

Moonlight State Beach

Visitors to this wide, sandy beach enjoy swimming, surfing, and fishing. Facilities include volleyball and tennis courts, recreational equipment rentals, and a snack bar. The beach takes its name from the fact that local residents traditionally came here for nighttime picnics early in this century. Exit Interstate 5 at Encinitas Blvd. and proceed west to the state beach. (619) 729-8947.

Huntington State Beach.

(Left): Casa Estudillo, Old Town San Diego State Historic Park. (Below): Stevenson House garden, Monterey State Historic Park.

California of the Spanish and Mexican Eras

Spanish rule in California lasted little more than half a century, and Mexican rule only another 25 years. Considering that California's non-Indian population numbered just 9,000 by the end of the Mexican era, and considering that these 9,000 people were spread along some 600 miles of coastal hills and valleys from San Diego to north of Sonoma, the cultural and physical legacy of that short 1769-1846 span is impressive.

Spanish colonization took three forms: presidios or military posts, missions, and pueblos or civilian towns. Later, adobe houses appeared on land-grant ranchos of baronial scale. Many of the best-preserved and restored remnants of these early settlements are found in California's state historic parks.

In order of founding, the four presidios were San Diego, Monterey, San Francisco, and Santa Barbara. Serving as seats of civilian as well as military government until Mexican independence in 1821, they turned into the cities we know today by the same names. At one of those first presidios, in Santa Barbara, restoration, land acquisition, and reconstruction are resurrecting an important historic site right in contemporary downtown Santa Barbara.

Of the 21 missions founded by Father Junipero Serra and his fellow Franciscans, 19 remain. La Purísima Mission, in a completely undisturbed pastoral setting near Lompoc, has been largely rebuilt; its extensive grounds are enlivened by living history programs, as well as livestock and landscaping that evoke the feeling of California during the mission period. Mission San Juan Bautista stands directly adjacent to San Juan Bautista State Historic Park, which features a number of historic buildings and exhibits from the Mexican and Early American periods of California history. Sonoma State Historic Park includes a Mexican-period army barracks and a chapel that was built in 1840 on the site of San Francisco Solano, the only mission built during the Mexican Period. And Santa Cruz State Historic Park Preserves one of the original buildings that once made up Mission Santa Cruz.

Three pueblos were established as a result of formal governmental decrees: four others, including San Juan Bautista and Sonoma, grew up around missions. El Pueblo de Los Angeles, near the center of contemporary downtown Los Angeles, was stabilized and partially restored when it became a state historic park. Monterey State Historic Park contains some beautifully restored remnants of California's Spanish and Mexican period capital and main port of entry. Another example of a presidio-related pueblo is Old Town San Diego, which took shape when Spanish dominion ended and the presidio disbanded.

Other parks recall hacienda life. Los Encinos near Los Angeles preserves a natural spring and several 19th century buildings. Pio Pico State Historic Park commemorates Pio Pico, a wealthy *ranchero* who was the last governor of California under Mexican rule. Petaluma Adobe State Historic Park preserves the central house and headquarters of General Mariano Vallejo's magnificent 140,000-acre rancho in the Petaluma Valley. Sonoma State Historic Park preserves his much smaller American-period house, Lachryma Montis.

Two sites that are now state historic parks deserve special mention for their unique place in California history. Fort Ross, established in 1812, preserves an outpost of the Russian empire that caused the Spanish to worry about their hold on California. San Pasqual Battlefield State Historic Park preserves the site of a violent skirmish that occurred during the Mexican-American War of 1846.

Old Town San Diego.

(Top): Misty morning, Torrey Pines State Reserve.
(Above): Dory races at Torrey Pines State Beach.

San Elijo State Beach

Swimming, surfing, and picnicking are among the favorite activities along this narrow, bluff-backed stretch of sand. A nearby reef is popular with snorklers and divers, while its breakers attract surfers. One hundred seventy-one developed campsites are situated on the terrace above the 1½-mile long beach; a stairway connects beach and campground. Advance reservations for campsites are needed during the summer months. San Elijo State Beach extends along old Highway 101 (Route S21) ¾ mile north from San Elijo Lagoon's entrance channel, near the community of Cardiff-by-the-Sea. (619) 753-5091 or 729-8947.

Cardiff State Beach

This ¾-mile strip of level beach across from San Elijo Lagoon offers visitors a variety of coastal recreation, including surfing, swimming, surf fishing, and scuba diving. Cardiff State Beach is located off old Highway 101 (Route S21), between Cardiff-by-the-Sea and Solana Beach. (619) 729-8947.

Torrey Pines State Beach

This wide, sandy beach stretches 4½ miles, from Del Mar past Los Peñas-quitos Lagoon to the base of sandstone cliffs at Torrey Pines Mesa. Swimming, surfing, sunbathing, and fishing are popular activities here. The red-hued bluffs and their reflection in the wet sand make beach strolling a special treat at low tide. More ambitious hikers can walk from the Torrey Pines State Beach parking area to Scripps Pier in La Jolla, about five miles one way. Across the highway from the beach is Los Peñas-quitos Lagoon, an important breeding ground for many birds and fish now under the protection of adjoining Torrey Pines State Reserve. A picnic area and parking lot are near the entrance on North Torrey Pines Rd. (Route S21), about one mile south of Del Mar. (619) 729-8947.

Torrey Pines State Reserve

Torrey Pines State Reserve north of San Diego is one of only two natural Torrey pine habitats on Earth; the other is on Santa Rosa Island, 175 miles to the northwest. This 1,082-acre reserve was established in 1921, following nearly 40 years of effort by local citizens to protect the rare trees. Hikers follow trails through stands of wind-sculpted pines, past eroded sandstone bluffs to scenic overlooks high above the beach. Many visitors to this park come for the solitude and primeval wilderness quality of the setting—a rare commodity in urban Southern California. The reserve's rich plant community is a delight to botanists and the spring wildflower show is wonderful. Torrey Pines State Reserve also preserves most of Los Peñasquitos Marsh, one of Southern California's few remaining saltwater lagoons. A picturesque, pueblo-style structure that served as a restaurant when it was built in 1923 now houses a visitor center complete with interpretive displays. Vehicular access to the park is limited, so it is best to arrive early, especially on spring weekends. Picnicking and camping are prohibited in the reserve. The entrance is on North Torrey Pines Rd. (Route S21), south of Del Mar. (619) 755-2063.

San Pasqual Battlefield State Historic Park

The pastoral quietude of San Pasqual Valley was shattered at dawn on December 6, 1846, by a violent confrontation between Mexican and U.S. Army personnel during the Mexican-American War. General Stephen W. Kearny and his troops, weary after their grueling march across the Southwest from Kansas, their powder wet after an all-night rain, engaged Andres Pico and about 80 well-mounted *Californio* lancers in a running battle that lasted several hours. Combat resumed the next day at Mule Hill, resulting in a four-day standoff before U.S. Army reinforcements arrived from San Diego. Twenty-two Americans died and many others, including Kearny himself, were wounded. Pico's cavalry sustained only minor wounds. Nevertheless, hostilities in California ended a month later when Pico capitulated near Los Angeles. A new visitor center and museum present the action in video, maps, and dioramas. San Pasqual Battlefield State Historic Park is next to the San Diego Wild Animal Park, 30 miles north of San Diego, eight miles east of Escondido on Highway 78. (619) 238-3380 or 489-0076.

Old Town San Diego State Historic Park

Spanish occupation of California began in San Diego in 1769 with the establishment of a mission and a fort on the hill where Presidio Park is located today. Although the mission moved inland in 1774, the presidio remained. Housing for the garrison (disbanded after Mexican independence in 1821) was built at the base of the hill where Old Town San Diego State Historic Park is today. Built around a central plaza, the park contains many restored or replicated structures that now serve as museums, shops, or restaurants. Visitors can view such showcase houses as La Casa de Machado y Silvas; La Casa de Estudillo, a mansion built around a romantic garden courtyard; La Casa de Machado y Stewart, simpler and full of artifacts that reflect ordinary, day-to-day life in California during the Mexican era; and La Casa de Bandini, once a hotel, now a restaurant. Other historic buildings in the park are a schoolhouse, a smithy, San Diego's first newspaper office, and a stable with a carriage collection. Additional shops and eateries in more recent structures enliven the scene. Outside the park are half a dozen landmarks dating from 1835 to 1857, as well as the Mormon Battalion Museum, and the venerable houses of Heritage Park. The Mexican era ended here when crewmen of the USS *Cyane* came ashore and ran up Old Glory in the plaza in 1846. (619) 237-6770 or 237-6766.

Silver Strand State Beach

This seldom-crowded beach is on the sandspit that forms the outer edge of San Diego Bay between Coronado and Imperial Beach. With 2½ miles of ocean beach and ½ a mile on the bay, Silver Strand State Beach makes a good destination for a family outing due to the bay's calm waters and ocean's gentle surf. It derives its name from the silvery seashells found on the park's seaward side. There is a picnic area and ample parking for day use. A campground and boat-launch facility will be added soon. Silver Strand State Beach is four miles south of Coronado on Highway 75. (619) 435-5184 or 237-6766.

Border Field State Park

This park at the extreme southwest corner of the continental United States contains an obelisk set into the border fence that marks the international boundary established with Mexico by the Treaty of Guadalupe Hidalgo in 1848. Three hundred of Border Field State Park's 680 acres lie within the 2,500-acre Tijuana River National Estuarine Reserve, one of the most nearly natural estuarine environments in Southern California. Birders, hikers, and equestrians use its network of trails to explore the salt marsh and adjacent beach. It is home to several endangered birds and plants and scores of other species. A new visitor center features a number of exhibits about the natural history of this unique environment. To reach the park, go south on Interstate 5 from Imperial Beach, turn south on Hollister St., then west on Monument Rd. (619) 237-6766.

Decorative cart, Bazaar Del Mundo, Old Town San Diego State Historic Park.

CHAPTER SIX

Southern California Inland

Inland Southern California is one of the state's most geographically diverse regions. A greater cross section of native plant and wildlife communities are compressed into this area than perhaps any other part of the state. The western valleys and foothills are cloaked with chaparral and oak woodlands that are rapidly giving way to urban development. Running through the heart of the region in the shape of a broad, rumpled arc, are 20 distinct mountain groups that make up the Transverse and Peninsular ranges. These mountains constitute Southern California's primary watershed and contain a number of high-elevation botanical "islands" mantled with pine forest. To the east, in the rain shadow of the mountains, are the great—and fascinating—expanses of the Mojave and Colorado deserts.

The Mojave, or high desert, has five state parks, each reflecting a different aspect of this arid terrain. Providence Mountains State Recreation Area features underground caverns, rhyolite crags, and pinyon woodlands. Located in the western Mojave, Red Rock Canyon State Park is best known for its colorful sedimentary rock formations; it is also home to a remarkable variety of high-desert plants and animals. Closer to Los Angeles, the sprawling Antelope Valley contains a 2,800-acre site protecting the Joshua tree at Saddleback Butte State Park, an Indian museum displaying artifacts from early civilizations of the Southwest, and a preserve for the state flower, the California poppy.

On or near Interstate 5 in the Tehachapi Mountains four state parks offer a wide range of recreational opportunities. Near the top of Tejon Pass is a state historic park that preserves the remnants of an 1850s U.S. Army outpost called Fort Tejon. Close by is Hungry Valley State Vehicular Recreation Area, where camping and off-road vehicle riding are popular. On the south slope of the mountains are Pyramid and Castaic Lakes, California State Water Project reservoirs where boating, fishing, and camping can be enjoyed.

South and east of Los Angeles are five parks, two of which—Chino Hills and California Citrus State Historic Park—are relatively new and still largely undeveloped. The other three are state recreation areas at Lake Elsinore, Lake Perris, and Silverwood Lake where fishing, boating, and camping are the main attractions.

Three high-elevation state parks are found in the oak and conifer forests of the Peninsular Range: Mount San Jacinto, Palomar Mountain, and Cuyamaca Rancho. This 900-mile-long mountain system starts at the tip of Baja California and comes to a climax in Riverside County at 10,804-foot Mount San Jacinto—the highest peak in the range and namesake of the 13,000-acre state park. All three parks have excellent camping facilities; San Jacinto and Cuyamaca Rancho feature miles of hiking trails through scenic wilderness areas.

Five state parks in the Colorado Desert (a division of the much larger Sonoran Desert), or low desert, draw thousands of visitors each year in pursuit of recreation and warm winter weather. Least developed of the five is Indio Hills, where native palm oases flourish along the San Andreas fault west of Palm Springs. Further south, the immense Salton Sea lures boaters and anglers with its 360 square-mile surface. South and west of the Coachella Valley's lush citrus and date orchards is the eastern boundary of California's premier desert state park—Anza-Borrego. This 600,000-acre park has large tracts of wilderness, hundreds of miles of trails and roads, and an incomparable variety of unspoiled desert landscapes, including palm canyons, pinyon forests, wildly eroded badlands, hidden springs, and cactus gardens that explode into color when winter rainfall is adequate. Adjacent to Anza-Borrego is Ocotillo Wells State Vehicular Recreation Area, a 14,600-acre playground for off-road vehicle enthusiasts. Picacho State Recreation Area, a winter haven for boaters and campers, provides access to a scenic 50-mile stretch of the lower Colorado River.

(Left): Anza-Borrego Desert State Park. (Above): Cuyamuca Ranch State Park.

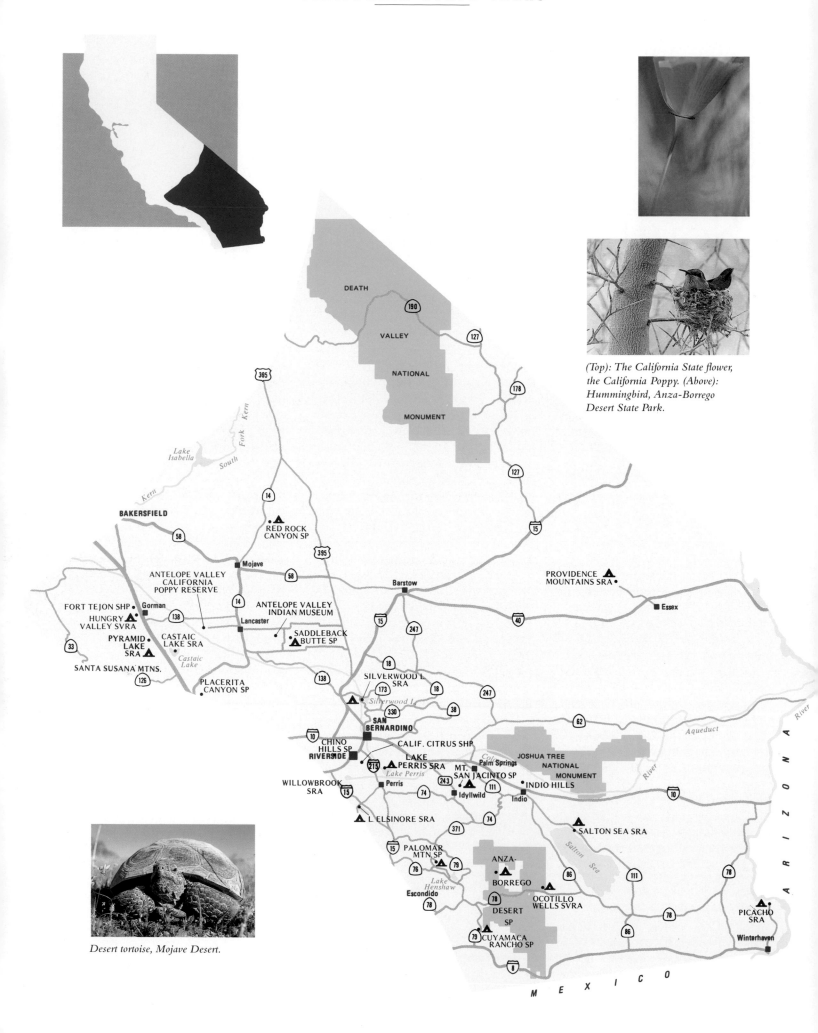

(Top): *The California State flower, the California Poppy. (Above): Hummingbird, Anza-Borrego Desert State Park.*

DEATH

VALLEY

NATIONAL

MONUMENT

190
127
178
127
15
40

385

Lake Isabella

South Fork Kern

Kern

14

BAKERSFIELD

58

RED ROCK CANYON SP
US 395

Mojave

58

Barstow

PROVIDENCE MOUNTAINS SRA

Essex

ANTELOPE VALLEY CALIFORNIA POPPY RESERVE

14

ANTELOPE VALLEY INDIAN MUSEUM

FORT TEJON SHP
Gorman
138
Lancaster

HUNGRY VALLEY SVRA

CASTAIC LAKE SRA

PYRAMID LAKE SRA

33

Castaic Lake

SANTA SUSANA MTNS.

126

PLACERITA CANYON SP

SADDLEBACK BUTTE SP

138

18

247

SILVERWOOD L. SRA

173

18

330

247

38

Silverwood L.

SAN BERNARDINO

62

Aqueduct

ARIZONA

River

CHINO HILLS SP

RIVERSIDE

10

CALIF. CITRUS SHP

LAKE PERRIS SRA

215

Lake Perris

Perris

WILLOWBROOK SRA

15

74

Col.
Palm Springs

JOSHUA TREE NATIONAL MONUMENT

MT. SAN JACINTO SP

243

111

Idyllwild

Indio

INDIO HILLS

10

L. ELSINORE SRA

371

74

SALTON SEA SRA

PALOMAR MTN. SP

15

76

79

ANZA-

Salton Sea

111

78

Escondido

Lake Henshaw

BORREGO

86

PICACHO SRA

78

OCOTILLO WELLS SVRA

78

DESERT SP

79

CUYAMACA RANCHO SP

86

Winterhaven

8

MEXICO

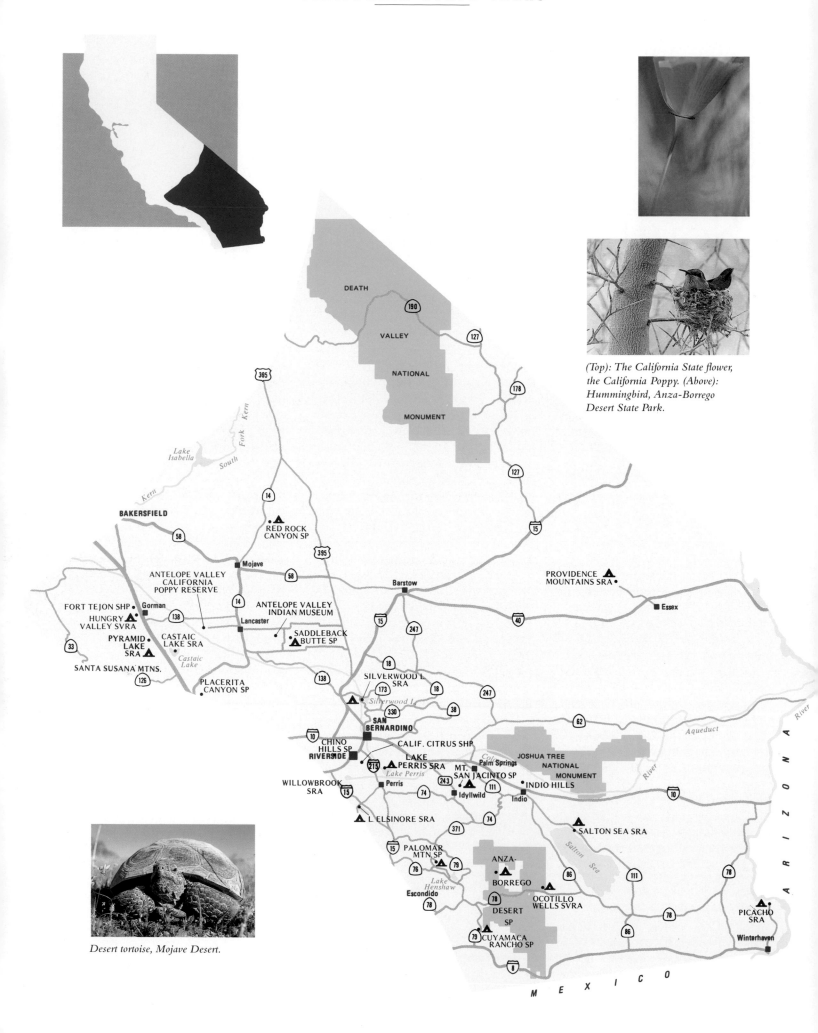

Desert tortoise, Mojave Desert.

Mojave Desert

Antelope Valley California Poppy Reserve

After the winter and spring rains, a brilliant carpet of color spreads across the floor of this 1,745-acre high-desert area as the golden poppy, California's state flower, and other wildflowers burst into bloom. A charming little interpretive center is open during the spring (March through early May). It features natural history displays including the watercolor paintings of Jane Pinheiro, who was a leader in the effort to preserve a portion of this area. It is also the starting point for seven miles of trail through the flower fields. The reserve is near Lancaster on Lancaster Rd. (an extension of Ave. I), 15 miles west of Highway 14. (805) 724-1180 or 942-0662.

Antelope Valley Indian Museum

Literally carved into the bedrock of Piute Butte, this handcrafted, chalet-style house is the site of the Antelope Valley Indian Museum. The artist, Howard Arden Edwards, acquired this land under the Homestead Act and began building the house in 1928. He filled it with his extensive collection of artifacts from aboriginal and contemporary California and Southwestern native cultures. In 1938 Edwards sold out to anthropologist Grace Oliver who added her collection to Edwards' and made the property into a museum that she continued to operate until 1979 when she sold the property to the state. The museum is located 2½ miles southwest of Saddleback Butte State Park on East Ave. M, between 170th and 150th streets. Call for hours and reservations. (805) 942-0662.

Saddleback Butte State Park

This 2,875-acre park in the western Mojave includes granite-topped Saddleback Butte and preserves a fine parcel of Joshua tree woodland, a once-common plant community in the Antelope Valley. Park activities include hiking, camping, picnicking, and star gazing. Saddleback Butte State Park is home to a variety of high-desert mammals and reptiles, including the desert tortoise—a slow-moving resident occasionally spotted by observant visitors. A ½-mile

nature trail has interpretive displays about the curious Joshua tree and other elements of the high-desert botanical community. Two longer trails connect to form a four-mile loop that goes all the way to the top of the 3,651-foot butte, a full 1,000 feet above the surrounding valley floor. The campground has 50 primitive campsites, each equipped with table and cooking grill. A group campsite suitable primarily for tent campers can accommodate up to 30 people. The entrance is on East Ave. J and 170th St., 17 miles east of Lancaster. (805) 942-0662.

Red Rock Canyon State Park

Red Rock Canyon State Park is located where the southernmost tip of the Sierra Nevada converges with the El Paso Range. It is the site of some of the California desert's most colorful geological formations. Red Rock Canyon and the surrounding region were once home to the Kawaiisu Indians and their ancestors. Petroglyphs in the El Paso Mountains are the work of these people. The area was later inhabited by nomadic Indians of the Mojave Desert. From 1868 to 1875, a spring here became a stopping point for the famed 16 to 20-mule-team freight wagons that passed this way, carrying bullion from Cerro Gordo's silver mines south to Los Angeles and returning north, laden with supplies for the miners. The spectacular, eroded buttes and cliffs that are protected in today's park were one of the major landmarks used by muleskinners and others along this challenging route.

(Top): Joshua Trees in springtime at Saddleback Butte State Park. (Above): Badlands, Red Rock Canyon State Park.

Providence Mountains State Recreation Area

Prominent in the vast eastern Mojave, the rhyolite crags of the Providence Mountains form a dramatic 5,000-foot scarp to the west, while rising more gently on the east. Providence Mountains State Recreation Area protects 5,900 acres of this isolated and arid range, including the pinyon-covered slopes of 7,171-foot Edgar Peak. At an elevation of 4,300 feet, the park's visitor center offers sweeping views across the desert to peaks in Arizona, 85 miles east. Providence Mountains State Recreation Area is perhaps best known for the remarkable limestone caverns that are protected within Mitchell Caverns Natural Preserve. Guided tours of the caves are conducted daily, except in summer. Contact the park staff for information. The ½-mile Mary Beal Nature Trail helps visitors learn more about the interesting plants of the region. A trail up Crystal Spring Canyon leads to rugged slopes and vista points.

A primitive six-site campground with limited water is found near park headquarters. Another campground—with no available water—is located in the nearby Hole-in-the-Wall area (outside the park) and is operated by the Bureau of Land Management. To reach Providence Mountains State Recreation Area, drive 100 miles east of Barstow via Interstate 40, and exit on Essex Rd. It is 17 miles from the freeway to the visitor center. (619) 389-2303 or 389-2281.

North of Los Angeles

Fort Tejon State Historic Park

The Pedro Fages expedition of 1772 used this route over the mountains north of Los Angeles. The R.S. Williamson survey of 1853 mapped it and soon afterward the U.S. Army decided to establish a military outpost here that would replace Fort Miller near present-day Fresno. On August 10, 1854, 1st Lieutenant Thomas Castor of the U. S. Army's First Dragoons led the first detachment into camp at what soon came to be known as Fort Tejon. Situated near the head of Grapevine Canyon in the Tehachapi Mountains, Fort Tejon was intended to protect the Indians of the Tejon Reserve and to serve as a

police force for the Indian agent. The dragoons also enforced civil law when requested to do so by the civil authorities. Grapevine Canyon became the major north-south route—the "Grapevine"—between Los Angeles and the San Joaquin Valley. Wagons, stagecoaches, and later, motor vehicles used the route which became U. S. Highway 99 in 1933 and is now Interstate 5.

The park features several restored or reconstructed adobes from the original fort and a number of magnificent 400-year-old valley oaks. On the first Sunday of each month, the fort comes alive with volunteers in period dress performing some the activities that were common at Fort Tejon during the 1850s. Civil War battle re-enactments are conducted on the third Sunday of each month from April through October. To reach the park, use the Fort Tejon exit from Interstate 5, 76 miles northwest of Los Angeles. (805) 248-6692.

Hungry Valley State Vehicular Recreation Area

This 19,000-acre recreation area contains hills and valleys, grassland, coastal sage scrub, and oak woodland. It provides multiple trail and road choices for motorcycles, ATVs, 4WDs, and dune buggies. A zone system adds further variety. One zone covers a large expanse that is suitable for open riding and primitive camping in gentle terrain. The largest zone is used for trail riding only. It has 80 miles of marked trail, graded by degree of skill required. Another zone is reserved for clubs and special events. Camping is allowed on

(Below left): Red Rock Canyon. (Below right): Hungry Valley.

Visitors to this 4,000-acre park can explore a gorge, a natural amphitheater, and numerous tributary canyons—all intricately wrought in caprock ridges and fluted columns carved out of the varicolored, fossil-rich, tilted beds of the Ricardo Formation. The cliffs, whose colors range from white to vivid red, may seem familiar because of their frequent exposure in Western movies.

What was once the town of Ricardo, a busy stagecoach station during the area's 1890s gold rush, is now the site of park headquarters, Ricardo Ranger Station. Graded roads circle Red Rock's two natural preserves where flora and fauna of both the Mojave Desert and Sierra Nevada can be found. Overnight campers discover what photographers know: these rock bastions take on an added excitement in the light of early morning and late afternoon. Tables, stoves, piped-in water, and pit toilets are provided in the 50-site primitive campground. Interpretive programs are conducted during the spring and fall. Red Rock State Park is 25 miles northeast of Mojave on Highway 14. (805) 942-0662.

1,600 acres; there is no water provided, but there are chemical toilets. Along the park's north edge, ⅓ of the trail-only sector is set aside to encourage the recovery of native bunch grasses, once nearly eliminated by grazing. To the west, a 60-acre, hike-in natural preserve protects stands of valley oak and native grasses. To reach the park, exit Interstate 5 at Gorman, 68 miles northwest of Los Angeles. (805) 248-6447.

Pyramid Lake State Recreation Area

The gorge of Piru Creek now holds the dam that created this reservoir and drowned the most scenic portion of old U. S. Highway 99. Situated at 2,578 feet in a mountainous setting, Pyramid Lake features 21 miles of shoreline, much of it in narrow canyons with dramatic walls of tilted rock strata. Managed by the U. S. Forest Service, Pyramid Lake State Recreation Area has an eight-lane launching ramp, marina, and boat rentals, as well as several picnic areas—some of which are reached by boat. A concessionaire-operated campground contains 100 developed sites with hookups for water and electricity. Exit Interstate 5 at Hungry Valley Rd., 60 miles northwest of downtown Los Angeles. (805) 296-9710 or (818) 574-1613. Campground: (805) 257-2892.

Castaic Lake State Recreation Area

Castaic Lake is one of the State Water Project's largest recreational lakes and the terminal reservoir of its west branch. It has 2,235 surface acres, 29 miles of shoreline, and launching ramps on the south side of its dam. Below the dam a 197-acre lagoon offers swimming, small-boat sailing, and shore and boat fishing. The main reservoir has two arms which reach back into steeper canyons. The east arm is reserved for sailing, fishing, and slow boating, while the west arm is used for fast boating and waterskiing. Both lake and lagoon are stocked with warm-water species such as bass, catfish, and crappie. There are picnic and group-camping areas, and concessions for food, bait, and tackle, as well as boat rentals. The State Water Project Visitor Center offers a panoramic view of the lake. Castaic Lake State Recreation Area

is operated by Los Angeles County and can be reached by exiting Interstate 5 at Lake Hughes Rd., 41 miles northwest of downtown Los Angeles. From Ventura, it is 51 miles to Castaic Lake via Highway 126 and Interstate 5. (805) 257-4050.

San Bernardino and Riverside Counties

Silverwood Lake State Recreation Area

Silverwood Lake State Recreation Area is situated on the chaparral-clad desert slope of the San Bernardino Mountains. At 3,350 feet, it is the highest reservoir in the State Water Project. The lake's environs attract a wide variety of birds, including waterfowl, raptors, and songbirds. Around its 13-mile perimeter are picnicking areas (three of them boat-in), 12 miles of hiking trails, swimming beaches, and designated areas for boating, waterskiing, and fishing (trout, bass, catfish, and others). There is a marina with a launching ramp, boat and equipment rentals, as well as a store. Camping facilities feature 136 developed sites that can accommodate 34-foot RVs (no hookups), a dump station, three developed group camps and one primitive group camp. Access to the recreation area is from Highway 138, 11 miles east of Interstate 15, or 20 miles north of San Bernardino via Highways 18 and 138. (619) 389-2281 or 389-2303.

Chino Hills State Park

This 11,000-acre, undeveloped open space is nestled in the hills north of Santa Ana Canyon. Preserved here in the midst of urban Southern California are rolling, grass-covered hills, riparian habitats lined with oaks and sycamores, and what is thought to be the largest remaining native stand of Southern California black walnut trees. Chino Hills State Park is home to deer and coyote, and some less-visible creatures including bobcats and badgers. There are two miles of trail for hiking only, and 30 miles for joint use by hikers, equestrians, and cyclists; motorists may drive in on graded road as far as the park headquarters. Facilities include eight primitive campsites (with adjoining horse corrals), picnic sites, piped-in

Silverwood Lake State Recreation Area.

Backpackers at Mount San Jacinto State Wilderness.

water, and restrooms. The entrance is on Pomona-Rincon Rd., about 4½ miles north of the Highway 71 and Freeway 91 junction. (714) 780-6222.

California Citrus State Historic Park

This 400-acre holding at the southern edge of Riverside contains an actively producing 150-acre citrus grove including that universal and glamorous symbol of California agriculture, the orange. Still in the development stage, this park will feature exhibits, programs, and other facilities that will tell the story of Southern California's citrus industry. This park is located at 1879

Jackson St. (714) 780-6222.

Lake Perris State Recreation Area

Ringed by boulder-covered hills and low mountains, Lake Perris is the terminal reservoir of the State Water Project's east branch and is a popular destination for vacationers. With nine miles of shoreline, this 2,000-acre lake offers visitors an excellent variety of water-oriented activities including swimming, scuba diving, fishing (shore, pier, and boat), boating, sailing, and waterskiing. A paved trail for hikers and bikers circles the lake; several trails for hikers and equestrians enter the surrounding countryside, including one that leads to a scenic overlook at Terri Peak. Rock climbers head for the formations at the Big Rock area, just below the dam.

Picnic areas with tables, grills, and restrooms are found at Moreno and Perris Beaches and near Bernasconi Pass. Other facilities include a launching ramp, marina, boat and equipment rentals, snack bar, a store, and a waterslide. There is a large developed campground for tent campers and RVs; the RV section has hookups (no sewer) and a dump station, and can accommodate vehicles up to 28 feet long. There are two group camps and a primitive equestrian camp as well. Rangers lead interpretive programs in summer, including nature walks, hikes, fishing clinics, and Junior Ranger actvities. The Lake Perris Regional Indian Museum describes Native American life in Southern California. Lake Perris State Recreation Area is 11 miles southeast of Riverside via Highway 60 or Interstate 215. (714) 657-0676.

Lake Elsinore State Recreation Area

Indians called this shallow lake the "Little Sea;" 19th-century rancheros referred to it as Laguna Grande; the developers of a shoreside resort community in the 1880s named it Elsinore. Today, Lake Elsinore occupies a trough at the base of the steep eastern escarpment of the Santa Ana Mountains. The lake rises in periods of good rainfall and drops, or even vanishes, after prolonged drought. About five miles long by 1½-miles wide, Lake Elsinore gets heavy use by boaters. Waterskiers like its smooth morning waters, while boat

and board sailors catch the lake's reliable afternoon breezes. Anglers fish for bass, bluegill, catfish, and carp. At the lake's north end, entered from Riverside Drive, are a concessionaire-operated picnic area, launching ramp, 500-site campground (200 with electrical hook-ups), and dump station. Lake Elsinore State Recreation Area is located 25 miles southeast of Riverside via Interstate 215 and Highway 74. It is 30 miles east across the Santa Ana Mountains from San Juan Capistrano on Highway 74. (714) 657-0676. Campground: (714) 674-3177. Lake patrol: (714) 674-3005.

Peninsular Range

Mount San Jacinto State Wilderness and State Park

The majority of this park's 13,522 acres are protected as a state wilderness area. The park contains three peaks over 10,000 feet, including Mount San Jacinto, the highest point in the State Park System. Whether you arrive on foot or by tram, this park provides a wonderful opportunity to explore a majestic landscape of subalpine forest, granite outcroppings, and high peaks. San Jacinto's stands of lodgepole pine, its springs and meadows, and its chinquapin and deer brush thickets recall scenery of the Sierra Nevada. The mountain's high points offer breathtaking views over hundreds of square miles of nearby desert and mountain ranges. The northeast flank of Mount San Jacinto rises 9,000 feet in six miles, forming the steepest and most dramatic escarpment in North America.

From the east side, Mount San Jacinto State Wilderness is easily reached via the Palm Springs Aerial Tramway. This world-famous tram carries passengers 2½ miles up the mountain, beginning at Valley Station near Palm Springs. Climbing nearly 6,000 feet, the tramway passes above a succession of plant communities, ranging from the desert to high-altitude forest. Cool, pine-scented air greets disembarking passengers at the Mountain Station terminal, elevation 8,516 feet. Nearby is Long Valley Ranger Station, a picnic area, cross-country ski center, nature trail, and Desert View Trail. Mule rides complete with guide are provided by a concessionaire. Wilderness permits can

A young angler at Doane Pond, Palomar Mountain State Park.

be obtained at the ranger station for day use and for longer backcountry trips. There are four primitive trail camps in the park and some people hike clear through to Idyllwild on the west. Securing a wilderness permit in advance is recommended in summer. Between December and April, when snowfall and severe weather are common on the mountaintop, backpackers headed into the wilderness should come fully equipped for winter camping.

From the west, park visitors can begin their hike into the high country at Idyllwild. Mount San Jacinto State Park headquarters is located here, as well as Idyllwild Campground, with 31 developed campsites that can accommodate vehicles up to 24 feet long. Stone Creek Campground is six miles north of Idyllwild on Highway 243 and contains 50 primitive campsites as well as a trailhead for hikes into Mount San Jacinto State Wilderness. In summer, interpretive programs are held at both the Stone Creek and Idyllwild Campgrounds. (714) 659-2607.

Palomar Mountain State Park

Towering conifers and grassy meadows delight visitors to this mile-high park, just west of the world-famous Mount Palomar Observatory. In 1928, the builders of what was then the world's largest telescope selected 6,100-foot Mount Palomar for their observatory, citing the mountain's elevation above coastal fog, its clear skies, and its distance from the glow of city lights — qualities today's park visitors still enjoy. Palomar Mountain State Park preserves some of the finest coniferous woodland in the Peninsular Range; the forest here contains white fir, incense cedar, big-cone spruce, Coulter and Jeffrey pine, as well as five types of oak.

The 1,897-acre park has a fishing pond, an interpretive nature trail, trails into a natural preserve, celebrated views from Boucher lookout — and a sense of remoteness. The campground, valley, and pond are named after George Edwin Doane who homesteaded here in the 1880s; some of the apple trees he planted can still be seen. The campground has 30 sites, with picnic tables, cooking grills, and shower facilities. Access is from Highway 76, east of Pauma Valley up Route S6 (the "Highway to the Stars" built for Palomar Observatory), then left on S7 at a junction near the top. (619) 765-0755.

Cuyamaca Rancho State Park

By wringing moisture from Pacific winter storms, the 6,000-foot high mountains east of San Diego support a surprisingly luxuriant mantle of mixed coniferous and oak forest. Straddling this section of the Peninsular Range is 24,677-acre Cuyamaca Rancho State Park, a wooded high country with peaks, upland basins, meadows, intermittent streams, and Cuyamaca Lake. Over half of this former rancho is a designated wilderness area. Ranging from chaparral to yellow-pine forest, Cuyamaca's remarkable plant communities contain dense stands of cone-bearing trees, magnificent oaks, azaleas, and such rarities as the endemic meadow foam. This mountain environment is one of the few locales in Southern California where pronounced seasonal changes occur. In fall, black oak and other deciduous trees paint the hillsides with color, and in spring, the slopes are awash with myriad hues of green as trees and shrubs leaf out. Winter storms dust the mountains with snow and summer thundershowers can be spectacular.

With over 110 miles of trail to choose from, hikers and equestrians enjoy one of the most extensive trail systems to be found in a California state park. A fire road reaches the park's high point, 6,512-foot Cuyamaca Peak, which provides a view west to the sea, south into Mexico, and east over the desert. Another trail leads to the summit of Stonewall Peak, an area popular with rock climbers. Park visitors will find three sites that interpret Rancho Cuyamaca's rich human and natural history. Exhibits at the Stonewall Mine ruins near Cuyamaca Lake describe the gold boom that occurred here between 1870 and 1891. A visitor center at Paso Pichaco Campground features the park's natural history, and the museum at park headquarters tells the story of the Indians who lived here for many centuries.

Paso Pichaco Campground has 85 family campsites, four walk-in "environmental" campsites, and two group camping areas. Green Valley Campground has 81 family campsites. Vehicles up to 30 feet long can be accommodated at either campground; there are no hookups. There are also six trail camps, including equestrian campsites. Park headquarters is nine miles north of Interstate 8 on Highway 79, which exits the freeway 30 miles east of San Diego. (619) 765-0755.

(Left and Below): Rare and endangered desert bighorn sheep.

Protecting the Desert Bighorn Sheep

One of the most majestic animals inhabiting California parklands is the desert bighorn sheep. Unfortunately, these reclusive creatures have all but vanished from Mount San Jacinto State Park and need help to combat threats to their survival in Anza-Borrego Desert State Park, and Picacho and Providence Mountains state recreation areas. Today, desert bighorn sheep are the focus of an extensive and unprecendented wildlife conservation effort.

Those concerned with the plight of the bighorn may take comfort from the example of two California state parks committed to protecting animals that were once nearly extinct. Prairie Creek Redwoods State Park on the North Coast nurtures herds of Roosevelt elk, which have made a stunning comeback since they were nearly wiped out at the turn of the century. And on a last remnant of its original habitat, the once-abundant tule elk now have sanctuary in Tule Elk State Reserve in the southern San Joaquin Valley.

In California, the term "desert bighorn" includes two related races. Peninsular bighorn are primarily found along the eastern, or desert, edge of the Peninsular Ranges. Nelson bighorn are scattered in small herds throughout the Basin Ranges in the sprawling deserts of southeastern California. Their cousin, the rare Sierra bighorn, is not found in any state parks.

There are many impediments to the survival and eventual increase of desert bighorn sheep. Roads, fences, subdivisions, mines, and even campgrounds intrude on their range and may mean loss of habitat and disruption of lambing grounds. Off-highway vehicles create stress. Some sheep are still lost to poachers. Access to scarce water can be denied to bighorns by people camping near waterholes, by grazing competition from domestic or feral cattle and burros, and by the spread of tamarisk—a tree from the Middle East so aggressive and water-greedy it can dry up a waterhole. Apart from encroaching civilization, the greatest hazard to the bighorn is infection by livestock diseases to which they have little resistance. Such diseases often result in catastrophically high lamb mortality rates.

In Anza-Borrego, herculean efforts are underway to protect desert bighorn sheep. Some 300 to 400 sheep, two-thirds of the Peninsular bighorns remaining in the United States, range over that 25 percent of the park suitable for their habitat. In 1987, specially trained crews used helicopter and net guns to remove 111 feral cattle from that habitat. Fourteen miles of fence were installed to keep cattle out of bighorn habitat. Six guzzler systems were built to assure bighorns a summer water supply. Thirty acres of tamarisk were removed to restore waterholes. Sick lambs were captured and nursed back to health; these survivors will be capable of producing antibodies against exotic diseases. As the program continues, biologists inoculate bighorns against viruses with the aid of helicopters and air-powered rifles. Censuses are conducted from the air and on the ground and a research program is studying lamb mortality, sheep movements, and other data. As a result of the multi-faceted wildlife conservation program in Anza-Borrego, the sheep population is expected to stabilize and then grow.

Elsewhere the news is not so hopeful. In Mount San Jacinto for example, high-country cattle herds may be acting as a pool for diseases that have reduced a bighorn population of 350 to a tenth that number—and maybe even to zero. Mining activity in both Providence Mountains and Picacho state recreation areas threatens habitat beyond park limits. Bighorns in these areas will need help in order to survive. Both areas are "islands" of bighorn habitat with relatively low numbers of sheep. In such areas bighorn sheep are particularly vulnerable to disease, competition, and encroachment problems. Indiscriminate mining activities have been carried on in these two ranges for over a century. Feral burros imperil the bighorn in both ranges. Tamarisk groves restrict bighorn access to the Colorado River. Fortunately, tamarisk eradication experiments have begun at Picacho. And, it is to be hoped that the experience at Anza-Borrego will point the way to further success in bighorn preservation efforts.

Colorado Desert

Indio Hills Palms

Native California fan palms thrive in many locations but rarely in such numbers as in the canyons of the Indio Hills. Here, along a line where the San Andreas Fault captures groundwater that nurtures the palms, is a 2,206-acre wild parkland containing some fine palm groves, including Hidden, Pushawalla, Biskra, Macomber and Horseshoe palms. The nearest groves are relatively easy to reach from the new trailhead and parking area 4 miles north of Indio. For further information call the Nature Conservancy, which operates this park unit and the adjacent 13,000-acre Coachella Valley Preserve, as well as the Thousand Palms Oasis and McCallum Grove, east of Palm Springs on Thousand Palms Rd., 2.1 miles north of Ramon Rd. (619) 343-1234.

Salton Sea State Recreation Area

This broad inland sea, one of the largest in the world, was formed in 1905 when a dike broke during construction of the All-American Canal. Today it is 35 miles long, 15 miles wide, and has a 360-square-mile surface and 110 miles of shoreline. Salton Sea's low altitude—228 feet below sea level—results in atmospheric pressure that improves speed- and ski-boat engine performance. The sea's almost treeless edges are so flat that a stiff northwesterly breeze blows water onshore, sometimes adding ½ mile to the width of the sea's south end.

Great egret, Salton Sea.

Boaters, swimmers, bird watchers, anglers, and other visitors will find picnic areas, tamarisk-shaded campgrounds, marinas, docks, launching ramps, and a boat wash. The Salton Sea's waters are home to orangemouth corvina, gulf croaker, and sargo, all ocean transplants, and the uninvited tilapia, which come from nearby agricultural irrigation canals. Headquarters Campground has 41 developed sites, 15 of which offer full hookups. Mecca Beach Campground has 109 developed sites without hookups. There are also three primitive campgrounds along the recreation area's shore. From the park's visitor center, 25 miles southeast of Indio via Highway 111, Salton Sea State Recreation area stretches southeast for 18 miles. (619) 393-3052 or 393-3059.

(Top and Above): The desert's annual spring flower show at Anza-Borrego Desert State Park. (Right): Jackrabbit at Anza-Borrego.

Anza-Borrego Desert State Park

Established in 1933 as California's first desert state park, Anza-Borrego has grown to include over 600,000 acres, making it the largest state park in the contiguous United States. With over 500 miles of dirt roads, 12 wilderness areas, and many miles of hiking trails, Anza-Borrego Desert State Park offers vast opportunities for exploring the silence, solitude, and abundant natural wonders of the Colorado Desert.

Anza-Borrego is some 30 miles wide from east to west, reaching from water- and wind-sculpted badlands near sea level to the pinyon-juniper woodlands at 6,000 feet along the rugged eastern escarpment of the Peninsular Range. North to south, the park stretches 60 miles, from the Santa Rosa Mountains and lush riparian thickets along Coyote Creek to the dry, boulder-strewn canyons and washes near the Mexican border. The park takes its name from

intrepid Spanish explorer Juan Bautista de Anza, and from *borrego,* the Spanish term for desert bighorn sheep.

Although Anza-Borrego receives only a few inches of rain annually, it contains several oases, a number of year-round streams in verdant canyons, and, throughout the park, astonishing cactus gardens that burst forth with succulent green growth and showy wildflowers in spring. A truly remarkable variety of habitats and wildlife are found here. Attentive visitors can spot desert-dwelling creatures such as bighorn sheep, roadrunners, cactus wrens, chuckwallas, kangaroo rats, and countless other mammals, reptiles, and birds.

One of the first Europeans to explore this area was 39-year-old Anza who led expeditions across the region in 1774 and 1775 in his effort to establish an overland route between northern Mexico and California. Seventy-one

years later, Kit Carson, serving as a guide for General Stephen Kearny and about 160 American soldiers on their way to Southern California and the war with Mexico, followed a route that paralleled portions of Anza's trail through Anza-Borrego. Eventually incorporated into the Southern Emigrant Trail, Carson's route was used from 1858 to 1861 by the Butterfield Overland Mail to carry mail and passengers on its 25-day run from St. Louis to San Francisco. These early trailblazers and pioneers are commemorated at monuments found along the route in Coyote Canyon, Vallecito, and Box Canyon.

Modern-day travelers to Anza-Borrego may want to begin their visit at the park's excellent semi-underground visitor center, which features displays and slide shows on the region. The visitor center, open daily from 9 to 5 (except in summer), is located less than a mile west of the community of Borrego Springs.

Borrego Palm Canyon opens onto the desert floor just north of the visitor center; the nearby Palm Canyon Campground includes picnic grounds, 117 developed campsites, and a 1½-mile trail leading to the canyon's streamside groves of native fan palms. The only other developed campground in the park is Tamarisk Grove at the junction of County Rd. S3 and Highway 78. Tamarisk Grove is a 15-minute drive south of Borrego Springs and has 25 sites. Both campgrounds have picnic tables, shade ramadas, restrooms with adjacent showers, and interpretive nature trails. Trailers to 24 feet and RVs to 31 feet can be accommodated at both sites.

Primitive campgrounds are found in a number of scenic locations through-

out the park, including Culp Valley, Yaqui Well, Bow Willow, and Mountain Palm Springs. You must carry your own water supply when using these sites. Camping is also permitted alongside all park roads and designated routes of travel; campfires outside of designated campgrounds are strictly prohibited unless you bring a metal container and your own firewood.

When planning an extended back-packing or jeep trip in the park, it is advisable to purchase a guide book on Anza-Borrego. The park's jeep trails wind through beautiful washes lined with palo verde and smoke trees, into narrow, twisting corridors in the bad-lands, and across pinyon forests in the high country. Drive only on designated jeep trails—new tracks may take dec-ades for nature to erase! Jeep tours into the park are also conducted by private operators in Borrego Springs. And if you are prepared to hike, some of Anza-Borrego's most magnificent country awaits you.

Here is a sampling of favorite locales in Anza-Borrego Desert State Park that can be reached by most high-clearance, conventional vehicles: Font's Point for its sweeping overview of the fantastic maze of water-eroded hills in Borrego Badlands; Yaqui Well, with its fine bird watching and legends of lost gold; Box Canyon and Vallecito Stage Station (a San Diego County park), along the historic Southern Emigrant Trail; Bow Willow Canyon, with its campground, giant desert willows, elephant trees (rare this far north), and palm groves; Split Mountain, with its towering, ver-tical canyon walls and intriguing geologic history.

From the northwest, Borrego Valley and the northern portion of the park can be reached via County Rd. S22 and the spectacular Montezuma Grade. From northern San Diego County, take Highway 78, which passes through the quaint mountain town of Julian enroute to the central part of Anza-Borrego. From the city of San Diego, take High-way 79 through beautiful Cuyamaca Rancho State Park or take Interstate 8 which leads to the southern edge of the park. From the east, the park can be entered via County Rd. S22, Highway 78, or County Rd. S2 off of Interstate 8. (619) 767-5311.

Dry wash at Anza-Borrego.

Ocotillo Wells State Vehicular Recreation Area

This 14,600-acre recreation area—with another 28,000 acres slated for acquisition—is located southeast of the Anza-Borrego Desert State Park badlands. It is left largely undeveloped at the request of its motorcycle, ATV, 4WD, and dune-buggy users. The wash-and-ridge terrain includes such features as a butte with dunes and a sand bowl, a blow-sand dune, springs, and a camp on a former homestead site. Camping is permitted throughout, though there is no water. Fire rings and picnic tables are available in the more popular primitive camp areas. The adjacent town of Ocotillo Wells has supplies and services. The recreation area's access points are on Highway 78, 16 to 19 miles west of Highway 86. (619) 767-5391.

Picacho State Recreation Area

Lining eight scenic miles of the lower Colorado River near jagged Picacho Peak, this remote desert park attracts large numbers of visitors (except in summer) who come to camp, hike,

fish, and boat. The park is centered near the site of Picacho, a turn-of-the-century gold-mining town which had 2,500 residents in its heyday. Picacho State Recreation Area provides access to majestic desert scenery along 55 miles of river between Parker and Imperial dams. Boaters can explore Adobe, Taylor, and Island lakes, which are tule-lined lagoons where feral burros and other wildlife can be found. It is also possible to visit Hoge Rock and Nortons Landing, historic sites that date from Picacho's steamboat era. Beaver burrows line the banks, migratory birds congregate here in winter, and a variety of mammals, including desert bighorn sheep, are found in the rugged country back from the river. The main campground has 50 campsites with piped-in water, chemical toilets, and solar-heated showers. There are also three group camps, two of which are designed for boat-in use. To reach Picacho State Recreation Area, take the 24-mile desert road—mostly unpaved—north from Winterhaven. (619) 767-5311 or 237-7411.

(Top): Chocolate Mountains, Picacho State Recreation Area. (Above): Ocotillo Wells State Vehicular Recreation Area.

(Above): A sidewinder appears ready to strike at Anza-Borrego State Park. (Right): A Joshua Tree is dramatically silhouetted against a desert sunset.

California's Unique Desert Environment

Probably no land traversed by so many people by rail or car has been so little understood as the desert. Visitors and migrants from rainier, greener lands usually see it as desolate wasteland. Yet upon acquaintance, the desert eventually exerts a powerful spell, creating loyal converts who come to understand its climatic rigors as well as its pleasures.

Moisture deficit—10 inches or less of rain per year, plus excessive evaporation —defines desert and creates its principal survival problem even more than summer heat. Plants and animals persist by ingenious adaptations (of form, physiology, and behavior) to heat problems but also to problems of water and energy conservation. For example, seeds of annuals that erupt into showy wildflower carpets may lie dormant for years before the right amount and timing of rainfall causes them to sprout, bloom, and successfully produce seed. Cactus, agave, and other succulents store moisture in fleshy tissue that shrinks in dry months and expands in moist periods. The Joshua tree, Mojave yucca, and other desert native plants have waxy leaf surfaces that slow the loss of internal moisture. To better compete for limited water, the creosote bush injects a toxin into the soil to keep other plants out of the area where its shallow roots gather moisture. Palo verde, ocotillo and others drop leaves during dry spells, sprouting new ones after rain. The mesquite sends its roots deep into the ground to probe for water. The white leaves of desert holly reflect solar heat. Goatnut turns only the edges of its leaves toward the sun in order to minimize heat absorption.

Animals have adapted with equal ingenuity. Light colors reflect heat away. Heavy fur and fur-tufted feet insulate from hot air and scorching ground. The large ears of the kit fox and jackrabbit radiate body heat efficiently. Some animals have developed water-conserving kidneys and other internal mechanisms; indeed, the kangaroo rat does not drink at all, but gets its water from solid food. The Mojave ground squirrel and poorwill estivate, sleeping summer away at minimum metabolic and water-spending rates. Other creatures seek shade, retire to burrows at midday, or become active only from dusk through dawn, among them the cottontail, jackrabbit, kangaroo and wood rats, pocket mice, and their predators—snakes, kit fox, owl, and nighthawk.

A trouble-free hiking or camping excursion to a desert park starts with certain precautions. Never go into remote areas of the desert alone; let rangers or friends know of your itinerary. Always carry water, especially during the hot-weather months when daytime temperatures usually soar above 100°F. One gallon per person per day is recommended—more when hiking. Sturdy shoes, sun screen, a hat, cotton long-sleeved shirt, and long pants are recommended. This type of attire provides better protection from dehydration and spiny vegetation than tank tops and shorts. When camping or exploring the desert by car, carry a shovel, tools, a jack and spare tire, flares, extra water, and even blankets in your car. In case of a breakdown, it's usually best to stay near your vehicle since it is easier to spot from afar than a person.

In California's three major deserts—Great Basin, Mojave, and Colorado (a division of the much larger Sonoran Desert)—there are 12 state parks. Although the three deserts share many climatic attributes, they each feature their own unique plant and animal communities. A helpful introduction to the California desert can be found at any visitor center in a desert state park. Mono Lake Tufa State Reserve, located on the western edge of the Great Basin Desert, has a visitor center in the town of Lee Vining. In the Mojave Desert, Providence Mountains State Recreation Area and the Antelope Valley California Poppy Preserve (open seasonally) have excellent visitor centers. Anza-Borrego Desert State Park preserves over 600,000 acres of the Colorado Desert in San Diego County and boasts one of the finest visitor centers in the State Park System.

Further Information about California's State Parks

Information: For campsite reservations, call MISTIX at 1-800-444-PARK. For general information, contact California Department of Parks and Recreation, Public Relations Office, P.O. Box 942896, Sacramento, CA 94296-0001. Tel: (916) 445-6477. For California state park publications, contact the Publications Section at the above address or call (916) 322-7000.

Handicapped Access: Wheelchair accessible trails and other facilities are available in many state parks, and more are being constructed each year. Please call the park for specific local information.

Dogs: Dogs are welcome in state parks, but they must be kept on a leash at all times (6-foot maximum length) and in an enclosed vehicle or tent at night. Dogs must be confined to campground and picnic areas and are not allowed on trails or most beaches. A $1 fee is charged for each dog entering a park.

The Sno-Park Program: This program provides a number of specially designated parking areas for use by cross-country skiers, snowmobilers, and other snow recreationists. Permits can be purchased from participating winter recreation retail outlets, Automobile Associations, and selected state parks. For more information, write to California Sno-Park Program, P.O. Box 942896, Sacramento, CA 94296-0001.

Collecting: Flowers, rocks, plants, animals, artifacts, and other park features are protected by state law and may not be disturbed or collected. Driftwood may, however, be collected on some beaches. Please check with a ranger or other park staffmember.

Tide Pools: Marine invertebrates that inhabit the intertidal zones are protected except for certain species at certain times of year. A valid sportfishing license is required. Check the local sportfishing regulations for species, season, size, and bag limitation.

Riding and Hiking Trails: Hiking, bicycling, and horseback riding trails have been developed in most state parks. Contact the park for specific trail information.

Fires: Fires are permitted only in park stoves and fireplaces. Gas-type cooking stoves may be used unless the area is otherwise posted. You may bring your own firewood or purchase it in the park. Gathering firewood in the park is not permitted. Fireworks are not allowed and smoking is prohibited in some areas.

Hunting: Hunting or the possession of loaded firearms is prohibited in most parks. However, several state recreation areas allow hunting of certain species of game in some areas during specified hunting seasons. Before hunting, be sure to check with the individual park for any special restrictions that may be in effect.

Diving: For your safety and protection, diving is prohibited throughout the State Park system, except in specifically designated areas.

The California State Parks Foundation: Formed in 1969 to enhance, protect and expand California's state park system, the California State Parks Foundation (CSPF) has raised more than $77,000,000 in funds, lands and artifacts, and completed more than 55 parks projects around the state. Though it is not a formal part of the State bureaucracy, CSPF works on a close, cooperative basis with the Department of Parks and Recreation. CSPF provides funds to purchase land for new state parks, to build new Visitor Centers, or to restore priceless historical buildings. The Foundation responds to the varying needs of the many different parks while offering experienced fundraising assistance for the always evolving State Park System.

Over the past few years, CSPF has: opened the Sonoma Coast Trails Project, a lovely 3½-mile trail that meanders from the Sonoma hills to Sonoma Coast State Beach; provided support for the creation of White Oak Farm, a working turn-of-the-century ranch in Malibu Creek State Park; dedicated the Stagecoach Hills Azalea Preserve, a veritable "flower forest" of thousands of wild azaleas in every hue of the rainbow; and raised more than $350,000 to restore and open to the public Jack London's cottage in Sonoma County; as well as many other worthwhile and necessary projects.

You can join the California State Parks Foundation with a tax-deductible contribution and receive many membership benefits, including free day-use passes good at hundreds of state parks. Seniors ($25/year) receive 10 free day-use passes, a free state park guide folder, and *California Parklands,* the State Parks magazine. Family Members ($35/year) receive 15 free day-use passes, as well as all the Senior benefits. Frequent Visitors ($75/year) receive the magazine and an annual day-use pass, (good for a year from the month a member joins), which entitles them to unlimited visits to state parks for a full year. Touring Members ($100/year) receive the magazine, the annual day-use pass, and a free copy of the spectacular, full-color book, *California State Parks.* Life Members ($750) receive the *Parklands* magazine for life, and other recognition. Gift memberships are also available. For further information on the California State Parks Foundation, please write: CSPF, P.O. Box 5668G, Larkspur, CA 94939. Or call: (415) 461-2773.

List of codes for charts on pages 115–119.

A	Astronomical observatory
B	Bike trail
C	Park closed
D	Developed campsite
F	Floating camp
G	Golf
H	Hotel
Ho	Hostel
Hu	Hunting
L	Living history programs
P	Primitive campsite
R	Recreational building
Rv	RV hookups
S	Swimming pool
T	Theater
U	Undeveloped
Ws	Windsurfing
☐	Handicapped accessible

Note: Numbers under Group Campsites and Group Picnic Area indicate the number of Developed or Primitive sites—and the total capacity of all sites.

NORTHERN CALIFORNIA COAST

	Family Campsites	Hike or Bike Campsites	Environmental Campsites	Enroute Camping	Cabin Rental	Group Campsites	Trailer Sanitation Station	Picnic Area	Group Picnic Area	Food Service	Supplies	Boating	Boat-In Camps	Boat Launch Ramp	Boat Mooring	Boat Rental	Swimming	Fishing	Underwater Park or Reserve	Hiking Trail	Nature Trail	Horseback Riding Trail	Horse Camps	Interpretive Exhibits	Guided Tours	Visitor Center/Museum	Comments
Admiral William Standley State Recreation Area																		•									
Anderson Marsh State Historic Park							•											•		•	•			•	•	•	L
Angel Island State Park		9					•	4-480	•		•			•			•	•		•	•			•	•	•	L
Annadel State Park							•											•		•		•		•			B
Armstrong Redwoods State Reserve							•	1-150												•	•			•		•	B
Austin Creek State Recreation Area	25D,10P																	•		•		•		•			B
Azalea State Reserve							•														•						
Bale Grist Mill State Historic Park							•													•	•			•		•	L
Benbow Lake State Recreation Area	76D	1		•			•	•			•			•	•	•	•	•		•				•	•		
Bothe-Napa Valley State Park	49D	1			1D-30	•	•	1-60							•			•		•	•			•		•	B,S
Caspar Headlands State Reserve																		•		•							
China Camp State Park	30P	1		15			•	1-200	•		•			•	•		•	•		•		•		•		•	B
Clear Lake State Park	147D	2				•	•	2-120		•		•		•	•		•	•		•	•			•	•	•	
Del Norte Coast Redwoods State Park	145D	2				•	•	1-100										•		•				•	•		
Fort Humboldt State Historic Park							•														•			•	•	•	
Fort Ross State Historic Park	25P						•													•	•			•	•	•	L
Grizzly Creek Redwoods State Park	30D	•	6			1D-40	•	1-40						•	•		•	•		•				•	•	•	
Harry A. Merlo State Recreation Area						1D-150					•		•					•									Hu
Hendy Woods State Park	92D						•	•						•	•		•	•		•	•			•			B
Humboldt Lagoons State Park	30P		6					•				•	•	•	•			•		•							
Humboldt Redwoods State Park	245D,23P	9	5	•		2D-225	•	•	2-150		•			•	•		•	•		•	•	•	•	•	•	•	B
Jack London State Historic Park							•													•	•			•	•	•	B
Jedediah Smith Redwoods State Park	108D	5					•	•						•	•		•	•		•				•	•	•	
Jughandle State Reserve							•													•	•			•			
Kruse Rhododendron State Reserve																				•	•						
Lakes Earl and Talawa		8					•				•		•					•		•	•	•		•			B
Little River State Beach																		•									
MacKerricher State Park	142D,10P	1					•	•				•					•	•		•	•			•	•		B
Manchester State Beach	46P	1	10			1D-40	•										•	•		•	•			•	•		
Mendocino Headlands State Park																		•		•				•		•	
Mendocino Woodlands Outdoor Center				•														•									
Montgomery Woods State Reserve							•													•	•						
Mount Tamalpais State Park	16D		6	32	•	2D-95	•	1-60	•									•		•		•		•		•	B
Olompali State Historic Park																											C
Patrick's Point State Park	123D	6				1D-150	•	1-150										•		•				•	•	•	
Paul M. Dimmick Wayside Campground	28P						•										•	•									
Pelican State Beach																		•									
Petaluma Adobe State Historic Park							•																	•	•	•	L
Prairie Creek Redwoods State Park	102D	9	6				•	•										•		•				•	•	•	
Reynolds Wayside Campground																		•									
Richardson Grove State Park	169D	2				1D-50	•			•	•	•		•	•		•	•		•				•	•	•	
Robert Louis Stevenson State Park							•													•							
Russian Gulch State Park	30D	1				1D-40	•										•	•	•	•		•	•	•	•	•	B,R
Salt Point State Park	109D,20P	12	5	•		1D-40	•	•				•		•			•	•	•	•	•	•		•		•	B
Samuel P. Taylor State Park	60D	1		•		3D-125	•	•	2-125									•		•	•	•	•	•		•	B
Schooner Gulch							•											•		•							
Sinkyone Wilderness State Park	51P						•											•		•	•			•		•	
Smithe Redwoods State Reserve																		•		•				•			
Sonoma Coast State Beach	129D,27P	6	11	40			•	•				•		•			•	•		•				•			B
Sonoma State Historic Park							•																	•	•	•	
Standish-Hickey State Recreation Area	169D	1					•							•	•		•	•		•				•	•		
Sugarloaf Ridge State Park	50D					1D-50	•													•	•	•	•	•	•	•	B

	Family Campsites	Hike or Bike Campsites	Environmental Campsites	Enroute Camping	Cabin Rental	Group Campsites	Trailer Sanitation Station	Picnic Area	Group Picnic Area	Food Service	Supplies	Boating	Boat-In Camps	Boat Launch Ramp	Boat Mooring	Boat Rental	Swimming	Fishing	Underwater Park or Reserve	Hiking Trail	Nature Trail	Horseback Riding Trail	Horse Camps	Interpretive Exhibits	Guided Tours	Visitor Center/Museum	Comments
NORTHERN CALIFORNIA COAST (Continued)																											
Tomales Bay State Park		12				1D-40		•	2-64								•	•		•	•			•	•		
Trinidad State Beach								•									•	•			•			•			B
Van Damme State Park	74D	1	10	•		1D-50	•	•									•	•	•	•	•			•	•	•	
Westport-Union Landing State Beach	130P																•	•			•			•	•		
NORTHERN CALIFORNIA INLAND																											
Ahjumawi Lava Springs State Park		10						•										•		•							
Auburn State Recreation Area	20D,100P							•				•		•			•	•		•		•					
Benicia Capitol State Historic Park																								•	•	•	L
Benicia State Recreation Area								•									•			•				•	•		B
Bidwell Mansion State Historic Park																								•	•	•	
Bidwell River Park Project								•				•		•			•	•		•							
Burton Creek State Park																		•									U
California State Capitol Museum																					•			•	•	•	L
California State Railroad Museum																								•	•	•	T
Castle Crags State Park	64D		6					•									•	•		•	•			•		•	
Clay Pit State Vehicular Recreation Area																											U
Colusa-Sacramento River State Recreation Area	22D		•				•	•				•		•			•	•		•				•	•		
Delta Meadows River Park										•								•		•				•			U
D.L. Bliss State Park	168D	1				1D-150	•	•									•	•		•	•			•			
Donner Memorial State Park	154D							•									•	•		•	•			•	•	•	
Emerald Bay State Park	100D							•				•	•				•	•		•				•	•	•	
Empire Mine State Historic Park								•										•		•	•			•	•	•	B,R,L
Folsom Lake State Recreation Area	182D	1	3			2D-100	•	•	1-125	•		•		•	•	•	•	•		•	•	•		•			B,R,Ws
Governor's Mansion																								•	•	•	L
Grover Hot Springs State Park	76D							•									•	•		•	•			•			S
Irvine-Finch River Access Site								•			•	•		•				•						•			
Kings Beach State Recreation Area								•			•						•	•									
Lake Oroville State Recreation Area	137D		4			8D-225		•	3-200	•	•	•	•	•	•	•	•	•		•	•	•		•		•	F,R,Rv,Ws
Lake Valley State Recreation Area										•																	G
Malakoff Diggins State Historic Park	30D		5		•	1D-50		•			•						•	•		•		•		•	•	•	B
Marshall Gold Discovery State Historic Park								•	2-240									•		•	•			•		•	
McArthur-Burney Falls Memorial State Park	128D		6	•			•	•		•	•		•		•		•	•		•	•			•		•	
Old Sacramento State Historic Park								•	•															•		•	T
Plumas-Eureka State Park	67D					1D-30	•	•										•		•	•			•		•	B
Shasta State Historic Park								•																•	•	•	
South Yuba River Project	16D,2P							•					•				•	•		•	•						
Stanford House State Historic Park																								•	•		
State Indian Museum																								•		•	
Sugar Pine Point State Park	150D					10D-400	•	•				•					•	•		•	•			•	•	•	B,L
Sutter's Fort State Historic Park																								•		•	L
Tahoe State Recreation Area	38D							•			•						•	•									
Washoe Meadows State Park																		•									
Weaverville Joss House State Historic Park																								•	•	•	
William B. Ide Adobe								•										•						•	•		
Woodland Opera House State Historic Park*																								•	•		T
Woodson Bridge State Recreation Area	46D					1D-40	•	•				•	•				•	•		•	•			•	•		
CENTRAL CALIFORNIA COAST																											
Andrew Molera State Park	36P	•															•	•		•	•						
Año Nuevo State Reserve																		•	•		•			•	•	•	
Asilomar State Beach and Conference Center																	•				•			•	•		H
Bean Hollow State Beach								•										•			•						
Big Basin Redwoods State Park	188D	46			•	5D-250	•	•	1-250	•	•							•		•	•	•	•	•	•	•	B,Ws

*Not operated by the State of California.

CENTRAL CALIFORNIA COAST (Continued)

	Family Campsites	Hike or Bike Campsites	Environmental Campsites	Enroute Camping	Cabin Rental	Group Campsites	Trailer Sanitation Station	Picnic Area	Group Picnic Area	Food Service	Supplies	Boating	Boat-In Camps	Boat Launch Ramp	Boat Mooring	Boat Rental	Swimming	Fishing	Underwater Park or Reserve	Hiking Trail	Nature Trail	Horseback Riding Trail	Horse Camps	Interpretive Exhibits	Guided Tours	Visitor Center/Museum	Comments
Butano State Park	40D	6						•												•				•	•	•	
Candlestick Point State Recreation Area								•	4-80								•			•				•		•	
Carmel River State Beach																	•			•							
Castle Rock State Park		23						•												•	•			•			B
Cayucos State Beach												•						•									
The Forest of Nisene Marks State Park		6						•												•							B
Fremont Peak State Park	25P					3D-115		•	2-60											•	•			•			A
Garrapata State Park																	•			•							
Gray Whale Cove State Beach																	•			•							
Half Moon Bay State Beach	51D	4	•			1D-50	•	•									•			•		•					B
Hearst San Simeon State Historical Monument										•														•	•	•	
Henry Cowell Redwoods State Park	112D	1						•	1-400	•										•	•			•	•	•	B
Hollister Hills State Vehicular Recreation Area	150D					GD-1000		•	1-200											•	•			•			
Julia Pfeiffer Burns State Park			2					•											•	•							
La Purisima Mission State Historic Park								•												•		•		•	•	•	L
Lighthouse Field State Beach																								•			
Los Osos Oaks State Reserve																				•							
Manresa State Beach	83D																•	•		•	•			•			
Marina State Beach								•									•	•			•						
Montana de Oro State Park	50P	4	•					•										•		•		•	•	•	•	•	B
Montara State Beach																	•	•		•		•					B
Monterey State Beach																	•										
Monterey State Historic Park								•		•														•	•	•	
Morro Bay State Park	115D	•		•		2D-80	•	•	2-150	•		•		•	•	•	•	•		•				•		•	Rv,G
Morro Strand State Beach	104D							•									•	•									
Moss Landing State Beach			50														•					•					
Natural Bridges State Beach								•									•	•			•			•	•		Ws
New Brighton State Beach	114D	•		•			•	•	1-200								•	•			•			•	•		
Pacifica State Beach																	•	•									
Pescadero State Beach								•									•	•		•				•			
Pfeiffer Big Sur State Park	218D	1			•	2D-100	•	•	3-300	•	•						•	•		•	•			•	•	•	B,S
Pigeon Point Lighthouse																									•		Ho
Pismo Dunes State Vehicular Recreation Area	500P						•										•	•		•		•			•		
Pismo State Beach	143D	•					•	•		•							•	•		•	•	•			•		Rv,G
Point Lobos State Reserve								•											•	•	•			•	•	•	
Point Montara Light Station																											Ho
Point Sal State Beach																	•										
Point Sur State Historic Park																								•	•		
Pomponio State Beach								•									•										
Portola State Park	53D	6				2D-100		•	1-150											•	•			•		•	
Robert W. Crown Memorial State Beach*								•	•								•	•						•	•	•	B,Ws
Salinas River State Beach																	•					•					
San Bruno Mountain State Park*								•	•											•	•						
San Gregorio State Beach								•										•									
San Juan Bautista State Historic Park								•																•	•		L
San Simeon State Beach	134D,70P	2	•				•	•			•						•	•						•	•		
Santa Cruz Mission State Historic Park																											C
Seacliff State Beach	26D				•			•	1-120	•	•						•	•						•	•	•	Rv
Sunset State Beach	90D	•		•		1D-200		•	1-50						•	•				•	•			•	•		
Twin Lakes State Beach										•							•	•		•							
Wilder Ranch State Park																		•		•	•	•	•	•	•		B,L
William Randolph Hearst Memorial State Beach								•	1-200	•	•	•					•	•						•	•		

*Not operated by the State of California.

CENTRAL CALIFORNIA COAST (Continued)	Family Campsites	Hike or Bike Campsites	Environmental Campsites	Enroute Camping	Cabin Rental	Group Campsites	Trailer Sanitation Station	Picnic Area	Group Picnic Area	Food Service	Supplies	Boating	Boat-In Camps	Boat Launch Ramp	Boat Mooring	Boat Rental	Swimming	Fishing	Underwater Park or Reserve	Hiking Trail	Nature Trail	Horseback Riding Trail	Horse Camps	Interpretive Exhibits	Guided Tours	Visitor Center/Museum	Comments
Zmudowski State Beach																		•				•					
CENTRAL CALIFORNIA INLAND																											
Bethany Reservoir State Recreation Area								•			•			•			•										B,Ws
Bodie State Historic Park																								•		•	
Brannan Island State Recreation Area	102D	2				6D-180	•	•	4-200			•	•	•			•	•		•				•	•	•	Ws
Calaveras Big Trees State Park	129D		5			1D-125	•	•	2-400								•	•		•	•			•	•	•	R
Carnegie State Vehicular Recreation Area	50P							•		•	•													•	•		
Caswell Memorial State Park	65D					1D-40		•									•	•		•	•			•			
Colonel Allensworth State Historic Park	15D							•	1-80															•	•	•	
Columbia State Historic Park								•		•	•											•		•	•	•	B,R,T
Durham Ferry State Recreation Area*	75					100	•	•	100								•										
Franks Tract State Recreation Area										•							•	•									
Fremont Ford State Recreation Area																	•										
George J. Hatfield State Recreation Area	27P					1D-200		•									•			•							
Henry W. Coe State Park	20P	62	•			10D-500		•										•		•	•	•	•	•	•	•	B
Indian Grinding Rock State Historic Park	23D		5					•	1-100											•	•			•	•	•	
John Marsh Home																											C
Lake Del Valle State Recreation Area*	150D	4					•	•	8-500	•	•	•		•	•	•	•	•		•		•		•	•	•	Ws,Rv
McConnell State Recreation Area	21D					1D-110		•	1-180								•	•		•				•			
Millerton Lake State Recreation Area	131D	2				2D-100	•	•	2-200			•	•	•		•	•	•		•	•			•	•	•	B,Ws
Mono Lake Tufa State Reserve								•										•		•	•			•	•		
Mount Diablo State Park	60D					6D-180		•	3-130									•				•	•	•	•	•	B
Railtown 1897 State Historic Park						1D-50	•	•	1-350															•			T
San Luis Reservoir State Recreation Area	79D,20P							•				•		•			•	•						•			B,H,Ws
Tule Elk State Reserve								•																•			
Turlock Lake State Recreation Area	65D							•		•		•		•			•	•		•				•			
Wassama Roundhouse State Historic Park								•																			
SOUTHERN CALIFORNIA COAST																											
Bolsa Chica State Beach								•		•							•	•									
Border Field State Park								•									•	•		•	•	•		•	•	•	B
Cardiff State Beach																	•	•									
Carlsbad State Beach																	•	•									
Carpinteria State Beach	262D	4					•	•									•	•						•			Rv
Chumash Painted Cave State Historic Park																								•	•		
Corona Del Mar State Beach*										•	•						•										
Crystal Cove State Park			21			3D-120											•	•	•	•							B
Dan Blocker Beach*																	•	•									
Dockweiler State Beach*				•																							
Doheny State Beach	120D						•	•	6-1400	•	•						•	•	•					•		•	
Drum Barracks Civil War Museum																								•		•	
El Capitan State Beach	140D	4	•			3D-250	•	•		•	•						•	•			•			•	•	•	B
El Presidio de Santa Barbara State Historic Park																								•	•	•	L
Emma Wood State Beach		•		•		4D-120		•									•	•		•					•		B
Gaviota State Beach	59D	•						•		•	•	•		•			•	•		•				•			
Huntington State Beach								•		•							•	•									
Kenneth Hahn State Recreation Area								•										•		•							
Las Tunas State Beach																	•	•									
Leo Carrillo State Beach	164D	5	•			1D-66	•	•			•						•	•		•						•	Ws
Leucadia State Beach																	•	•									
Los Encinos State Historic Park								•																•	•		
Malibu Creek State Park	•	•						•				•					•	•		•		•		•		•	B
Malibu Lagoon State Beach								•									•	•		•				•	•	•	S

*Not operated by the State of California.

SOUTHERN CALIFORNIA COAST (Continued)

Park	Family Campsites	Hike or Bike Campsites	Environmental Campsites	Enroute Camping	Cabin Rental	Group Campsites	Trailer Sanitation Station	Picnic Area	Group Picnic Area	Food Service	Supplies	Boating	Boat-In Camps	Boat Launch Ramp	Boat Mooring	Boat Rental	Swimming	Fishing	Underwater Park or Reserve	Hiking Trail	Nature Trail	Horseback Riding Trail	Horse Camps	Interpretive Exhibits	Guided Tours	Visitor Center/Museum	Comments
Manhattan State Beach*																	•	•									
McGrath State Beach	174D	10					•										•	•		•	•			•			
Moonlight State Beach										•							•	•									
Old Town San Diego State Historic Park								•		•														•	•	•	L,T
Pan Pacific Park*								•																			T
Pio Pico State Historic Park								•	1D-60															•			
Point Dume State Beach*																	•	•									
Point Mugu State Park	56D,88P	12				4D-156	•	•									•	•		•		•		•			B
Redondo State Beach*																	•	•									
Refugio State Beach	85D	•				1D-60		•	1D-100	•	•						•	•		•				•	•		B
Robert H. Meyer Memorial State Beaches								•									•			•							
Royal Palms State Beach*																	•										
San Buenaventura State Beach								•		•							•	•									B
San Clemente State Beach	101D					1D-50	•	•									•	•		•							Rv
San Elijo State Beach	171D						•				•						•	•						•			
San Onofre State Beach	221D	26				1D-50	•										•	•		•							
San Pasqual Battlefield State Historic Park								•													•			•	•	•	
Santa Monica State Beach*										•										•							
Santa Susana Mountains																				•							U
Silver Strand State Beach			•					•									•	•									
South Carlsbad State Beach	226D						•				•						•	•									
Topanga State Beach*																	•										
Topanga State Park	8							•	•											•	•	•		•		•	B
Torrey Pines State Beach								•									•	•									
Torrey Pines State Reserve																				•	•			•	•	•	
Verdugo Mountains																				•							U
Watts Towers of Simon Rodia State Historic Park*																								•			
Will Rogers State Beach										•							•										
Will Rogers State Historic Park								•	3-300											•	•	•		•	•	•	B

SOUTHERN CALIFORNIA INLAND

Park	Family Campsites	Hike or Bike Campsites	Environmental Campsites	Enroute Camping	Cabin Rental	Group Campsites	Trailer Sanitation Station	Picnic Area	Group Picnic Area	Food Service	Supplies	Boating	Boat-In Camps	Boat Launch Ramp	Boat Mooring	Boat Rental	Swimming	Fishing	Underwater Park or Reserve	Hiking Trail	Nature Trail	Horseback Riding Trail	Horse Camps	Interpretive Exhibits	Guided Tours	Visitor Center/Museum	Comments
Antelope Valley California Poppy Reserve								•												•				•	•	•	
Antelope Valley Indian Museum								•													•			•	•	•	
Anza-Borrego Desert State Park	173D,200P					5D-175	•	•	3-75											•	•	•		•	•	•	B,Rv
California Citrus State Historic Park																											C
Castaic Lake State Recreation Area								•	1-500	•	•	•		•		•	•	•							•		
Chino Hills State Park	8P																			•	•	•	•	•	•	•	B
Cuyamaca Rancho State Park	166D,14P	10	4			3D-200	•	•										•		•		•	•	•		•	B
Fort Tejon State Historic Park						1P-150		•																•	•	•	L
Hungry Valley State Vehicular Recreation Area	150P					1P-300		•	•															•			
Indio Hills Palms								•												•	•			•	•		
Lake Elsinore State Recreation Area	150D,300P			•		4D-100	•	•	2-40	•		•		•	•		•										Rv
Lake Perris State Recreation Area	177D	1				6D-600	•	•	3-600	•	•	•	•	•	•	•	•	•	•	•	•	•	•	•	•	•	B,H,Rv
Mount San Jacinto State Park	33D,50P	1						•		•										•	•	•		•	•	•	
Ocotillo Wells State Vehicular Recreation Area	500P						•	•																•	•		
Palomar Mountain State Park	33D					3D-55		•										•		•	•			•			
Picacho State Recreation Area	50P					2D-100	•	•	1-50			•	•	•			•	•		•				•	•		H
Providence Mountains State Recreation Area	6P																			•	•			•	•	•	H
Pyramid Lake State Recreation Area*	60D					3D-75		•	•	•	•	•		•	•	•	•	•									
Red Rock Canyon State Park	50P							•												•	•	•		•	•	•	
Saddleback Butte State Park	50D					1D-30	•	•												•	•			•			
Salton Sea State Recreation Area	150D,1000P	5					•	•	•		•	•		•	•		•	•		•	•			•	•	•	Rv
Silverwood Lake State Recreation Area	136D	15				3D-300	•	•	3-240	•	•	•		•	•	•	•	•		•	•			•		•	B

*Not operated by the State of California.

Index